Wisdom

for the race of life

wisdom
for the race of life

Kriss
Akabusi
with Stuart Weir

Text copyright © 1999 Kriss Akabusi and Stuart Weir

The authors assert the moral right to be identified
as the authors of this work

Published by
The Bible Reading Fellowship
Peter's Way, Sandy Lane West
Oxford, OX4 5HG
ISBN 1 84101 004 9

First edition 1999
10 9 8 7 6 5 4 3 2 1 0

Acknowledgments
Biblical text is quoted from the *New International Version* of the Bible,
copyright © 1973, 1978, 1984 by the International Bible Society.
Published by Hodder & Stoughton. Used by permission.

A catalogue record for this book
is available from the British Library

Printed and bound in Great Britain by
Caledonian International Book Manufacturing Ltd, Glasgow

Contents

Introduction

What relevance can a collection of psalms and poems, written over 3,000 years ago in the Middle East, possibly have to people living in Britain today? I mean, David may have been a king but he didn't have a mobile phone or a web-site. He never travelled on the London Underground in the rush hour. He had not even heard of *Record Breakers*! So what insights could he have into the issues which concern modern society? A great deal, if you ask me...

In the early years after I became a Christian in 1987, my Bible reading was mainly the Gospels, Paul's letters and some of the historical parts of the Old Testament. Over the past few years I have come to know and love the wisdom literature in the Old Testament and have found within Psalms, Proverbs and Ecclesiastes real wisdom for my soul.

What I appreciate about the Psalms is that the authors write honestly about their experiences of the God they know, rather than attempting to write a theological treatise. He is a real God, one whom they have known in the past and in whom they have hope for the future. He is a personal God, a powerful God and a God who is relevant to every aspect of their lives.

The psalmists have a genuine relationship with their God. At times they sing his praises and express their gratitude. At other times they get angry with their God and they don't hold back from expressing that either. The bottom line is always that their God is accessible and that he is relevant to them in any situation.

If King David was suddenly transported from heaven

to Southampton today, the technological changes that have occurred in the past 3,000 years would blow his mind. A visit to my old army barracks would give him a few ideas for making even shorter work of Goliath than the sling and stones.

What hasn't changed much, if at all, in those 3,000 years would be people. The problems that concerned the psalmist all those years ago are still encountered in human society today. We still have hopes and fears. We have problems getting on with one another. We have wars and rumours of war.

We are still concerned about the uncertainty of life, the unpredictability of the future. These issues are addressed in the Psalms. Modern people, for all their knowledge and sophistication, still have the same spiritual needs and longings as the ancient Israelites had.

David, Asaph, Solomon, or whichever particular psalmist, feel strongly about these issues and they want to talk to God about them. They often express a concern that life is unfair. They have been faithful and have acted with integrity, yet God has not rewarded them.

So often as I read a particular psalm, I find myself thinking, 'I've been there. I know exactly what you mean.' I can recognize a situation from my own life. Whether it is the anger, the feeling of being misunderstood or mistreated by other people or by God, when the psalmist fails—like David so often did—I see myself. It is so easy for us to get it wrong, yet to want to blame God.

My Nigerian background gives further insights into the brutality of a Third World mind-set, the way of thinking we discover in the Psalms. We are very much protected from the realities of life here in the West. In a Third World situation you have to live much more by your wits.

My father is a Nigerian chief and, as his eldest son, I am the Crown Prince. My mother has often talked to me of the danger of one of my half-brothers usurping my authority, my position. But if they wanted to do the job properly they would have to get rid of not only me, but also my brother and my children. When we read in the Old Testament about a whole family being wiped out, it seems strange and brutal to us. But my background helps me to understand the mentality behind that.

The fact that my father is a chief also gives me insights into some of the things David says about being king. I can understand, for example, the political intrigues, the need to get people on your side if you are going to hold on to power. Understanding the 'bribery and corruption' mentality which is rife in so many Third World countries provides a helpful backdrop to some of the Psalms. As I observe how my father operates in his village, I see similarities to how David operates.

David is an interesting character. He is a man of contrasts. I admire David but in truth I don't like him. He is a murderer, an adulterer, conceited, arrogant, an extortioner. There are so many aspects of David which are unattractive. For example, how could David extort Nabal's goods, steal his wife and then go and praise God? (1 Samuel 25)

For me, however, David's saving grace is his faith in God. We are told that David was a man after God's own heart (Acts 13:22). I think the secret is that God was real to David. He had a real experience of God. There is a challenge to all of us to look at David's experience of God and to compare it with our own.

I find it helpful to use the Psalms as prayers. I like to read a line from a psalm and echo that in my thoughts to God. I read other bits and ask God to keep me from falling into the mistakes David made. Or I just read the verses through and meditate on them.

The amazing thing about the Psalms is that there is one for every occasion. You can read Psalm 8 and praise God for the wonder of what he has done. If you feel victimized and feel the need of vindication, read Psalm 109. It is all there.

There are several types of psalm, but they can probably be fitted into four main categories. There are psalms of declarative praise, in which the psalmist or congregation just wishes to declare the greatness, glory and majesty of God and give him the praise which he deserves.

There are descriptive psalms, in which the psalmist seeks to declare what God has done in his life personally, in the congregation, or even in the nation. In these psalms we find reference to God's creative ability, his presence and blessing on people, or the nation, over the years.

There are wisdom psalms, which often read like a series of proverbs, full of wise and pithy sayings. These psalms are full of truth—often subjective truth—and spiritual meaning. These are psalms where the psalmist wants to convey some very important, logical messages.

My fourth category of psalms is the lament, often written to describe deep times of trouble when the psalmist can barely keep his head above water. He may feel on his last legs, with nowhere to turn.

I have also included the Song of Moses from Deuteronomy chapter 32. While this is, of course, not really a psalm, it is a passage of scripture very much in the style of the Psalms. It is a powerful passage which has spoken to my own heart and which, I am sure, will have much to say to you.

The content of this book has its origins in a series of sermons preached at the Southampton Christian Fellowship during 1996–98. I am grateful to the pastor, Paul Finn, for the opportunity to preach, and to my fellow church members for putting up with me.

If you have never read the Psalms through, start today. It is my prayer that this little book may communicate to you some of the wisdom that I feel is to be found in the Book of Psalms.

Psalm 19

For the director of music. A psalm of David.

The heavens declare the glory of God;
  the skies proclaim the work of his hands.
Day after day they pour forth speech;
  night after night they display knowledge.
There is no speech or language
  where their voice is not heard.
Their voice goes out into all the earth,
  their words to the ends of the world.

In the heavens he has pitched a tent for the sun,
  which is like a bridegroom
    coming forth from his pavilion,
  like a champion rejoicing to run his course.
It rises at one end of the heavens
  and makes its circuit to the other;
  nothing is hidden from its heat.

The law of the Lord is perfect,
  reviving the soul.
The statutes of the Lord are trustworthy,
  making wise the simple.
The precepts of the Lord are right,
  giving joy to the heart.
The commands of the Lord are radiant,
  giving light to the eyes.
The fear of the Lord is pure,
  enduring for ever.
The ordinances of the Lord are sure
  and altogether righteous.

They are more precious than gold,
  than much pure gold;
they are sweeter than honey,
  than honey from the comb.
By them is your servant warned;
  in keeping them there is great reward.

Who can discern his errors?
  Forgive my hidden faults.
Keep your servant also from wilful sins;
  may they not rule over me.
Then will I be blameless,
  innocent of great transgression.

May the words of my mouth
  and the meditation of my heart
  be pleasing in your sight,
  O Lord, my Rock and my Redeemer.

This is a psalm which has been one of my favourites for some years. It is a lovely psalm.

David was a king, a warrior and a poet and, as we have mentioned, he was a man after God's own heart. When you read that sort of poetry, with such a depth of theology and love in it, you have to stand amazed at this man and see him as someone who obviously communicated with God.

The paradox is that we know that David was far from perfect. He was anything but sinless, yet he could sit down and write such wonderful poetry. I understand that dichotomy. Sometimes when I am in church I feel so good. I think, 'Yes, Lord, you are the main man in the house. You are God of all creation. You are to be praised and worshipped.' I wish I could be like that every single day of my life. But then I find that all those sinful thoughts which come into my mind come on my lips and come out in my actions.

That is what David is thinking when he writes: 'The heavens declare the glory of God; the skies proclaim the work of his hands.' Sometimes when David went outside, the heavens spoke to him about God's awesomeness and his glory.

'Day after day they pour forth speech; night after night they display knowledge.' Every day, he says, reveals the same message—that God is here and that he cares for his world. God's creation reminded David that wherever he went on the earth, God was there taking care of his people.

David looked at the sky and saw the awesome power and wisdom of the creator. There is no need for words. Neither the sun nor the moon need speak to you to express the glory of God. Their very existence says it all.

There is no language in which God has not spoken and declared his presence. This is a point which Paul picks up in his letter to the Romans:

'For since the creation of the world God's invisible qualities—his eternal power and divine nature—have been clearly seen, being understood from what has been made, so that men are without excuse.' (Romans 1:20)

Paul says that we can all know God from what we see in creation, that creation speaks to us about God. David articulates the same thought.

Children sometimes have more idea about this than adults: children see the stars and are fascinated; they see the wonder of creation and recognize that the sun was there before them. For the simple-minded, it is obvious that the creation speaks of a creator: 'In the heavens he has pitched a tent for the sun, which is like a bridegroom coming forth from his pavilion…' This is telling us that we are to be amazed by the sun and the moon but we are not to worship them. The sun has its limitations.

In the history of the world there have been many peoples who have worshipped the sun. Here, however, David is saying the sun is just part of the creation.

By the way, the background to this verse is that, in an Eastern wedding at that time, the bride might wait for days until the bridegroom decided to come out of his pavilion for the wedding to begin. See also the story of the wise and foolish virgins that Jesus told in Matthew 25; this story also describes the wait for the bridegroom.

The sun has a purpose. It brings the new day every morning. This was much more relevant in a more primitive society where they waited for daylight to start the day's work. Just like the wedding party rejoicing when the bridegroom appears, so the people rejoice when the sun appears.

I like the description: 'like a champion rejoicing to run his course'. I can remember when I was a champion ready to run my race. For a big race like an Olympic final, I had done all the training, all the hard work. When the time came to run the race, I was ready. I was excited. I was purposeful. I knew what my task was and I was focused on it.

David is saying that it is as if the sun rises and says, 'I'm ready to shine a new day in your life.' Every time you see the sun, you should thank God for another day to serve him and to touch people's lives.

What should our attitude to the new day be? Like a champion, be purposeful and focused on the main thing. Like a bridegroom, be ready.

We are not to worship the sun; we are not to worship the moon; we are not to worship the stars, but these things are to remind us of the creator and we are to worship him. As we contemplate these things, we should begin to ask: who is the creator behind these things?

David moves on from his thoughts on the heavens, recognizing that while these can help our awareness of God, they are not adequate methods of communicating the truth about God. So he continues: 'The law of the Lord is perfect, reviving the soul. The statutes of the Lord are trustworthy, making wise the simple.' Now he is going to give us a more theological insight into the creator.

In the first chapter of John's Gospel we read: 'In the beginning was the Word, and the Word was with God, and the Word was God. He was with God in the beginning.' (John 1:1–2)

Jesus was with God at the beginning. David did not know Jesus but he knew God's word, God's law. He knew that the Law of God was wisdom for the human soul. He knew that the Law of God was perfect, the one way of having sure knowledge of God. The Law helped him to know God and to know that God was truth.

I once came across a helpful illustration about coming to know Jesus. Imagine that at the end of your garden is a colony of ants. You enjoy watching them. The problem is that you know that the grass is about to be cut and the ants' whole world will be destroyed by the powerful electric lawnmower.

So every day you go down to the bottom of the garden and say, 'Ants, ants, you are in great danger. Your house is about to be destroyed.' You could even leave them a note, or put a big sign up. The problem is that the ants cannot understand you. Imagine, however, that in some miraculous way you are able to become an ant and go down there and warn them in their own ant language. Then they would understand.

Well, of course, we cannot become ants—but Jesus did become a man. He came into the world and told us that we were in trouble and offered us the way of escape.

'The statutes of the Lord are trustworthy, making wise the simple.' So many people walk around with so many ideas. But God says that his Law gives wisdom to the simple people, or, perhaps better expressed, to people who simply put their trust in him.

I firmly believe that any wisdom I have comes from what God has done in my life over the past few years. I read a great deal but I always try to remember that nothing I read should be allowed to take me away from my firm belief that wisdom comes from God. There are so many wise people—wise, at least, in their own eyes—who, as Paul put it in Romans chapter 1 verse 18, suppress the truth by their wickedness.

For some people, this can be summed up as worshipping the creation but not the creator. I believe, too, that many people are confused in their thinking by an uncritical acceptance of Darwin's theories of evolution. We suppress the truth so that we are free to do what we like. Many of those who believe in Darwin's theories of evolution get rid of the concept of the creator and are then free from moral constraints. What we think affects what we say and ultimately what we do.

There are so many wise people, clever people in our society. But if their wisdom is not from God, it will die with them. The psalmist reminds us that if we are prepared to be humble and admit that we are simple, God will give us wisdom.

'The precepts of the Lord are right, giving joy to the heart.' I remember when I was quite little, having to go shopping with mum. We went to the same shops in Kilburn every day and I did not want to go. One day I got a real strop on. I walked about ten metres behind her. I followed her but then I turned a corner and she was not there. I looked everywhere but she was gone.

Someone said to me, 'Are you lost, little boy?' I said, 'No, no, no!' and started walking round and round. After a little while, the same man asked again, 'Are you lost, little boy?' I said, 'Yes, I've lost my mummy.' He then took me by the hand and led me to my mum. I was so happy. For five minutes or so I had refused his help, refused to admit that I was lost. I had thought, 'I am the man in the house; I don't need help.' It was only when I was prepared to admit that I was lost that the man was able to help me.

There are so many people in our society who are spiritually lost. They say, 'No, no, no, I don't need any help. I am OK on my own.' They walk round in circles and always end up at the same place. Jesus says to them, 'Are you lost, little boy (or girl)? Take my hand; I will take you to the Father.'

'The fear of the Lord is pure, enduring for ever.' It does not change to suit you or me. It does not change to keep up with the latest fashions. It endures for ever. People's ideas come and go but God's wisdom has stood the test of time. Time and time again, I think I know better than God but each time I have to come back and admit that I was wrong—that I need God infinitely more than he needs me.

I wonder if there might be a revival just round the corner, because young people know that their parents have got it wrong? Young people see the futility of worshipping the creation rather than the creator. They have tried the words of mums and dads, teachers, pop idols and soap stars and not found the truth. My prayer is that they will look again at the Word of God.

'The ordinances of the Lord are sure and altogether righteous. They are more precious than gold, than much pure gold; they are sweeter than honey, than honey from the comb.'

Unlike us, God's Word has no bias, no 'shadow of turning', as the well-known hymn puts it. It is true and altogether righteous. It has no axe to grind. All it wants to do is show you and me how we can be in better communication with God. Money is good; I enjoy having money, but money is only good for today. God's Law is good for today, tomorrow and for ever.

There is a passage in the First Book of Samuel when King Saul had banned the whole army from eating until the battle was over and then Jonathan found a honey-comb and ate some honey and said afterwards, 'See how my eyes brightened when I tasted a little of this honey.' (1 Samuel 14:29) I am sure you know the situation where you haven't eaten properly one day, have skipped a meal or something. Then you eat a chocolate bar and you feel sustained, your energy restored. That is an illustration of what the Law of God does for your soul.

Honey is good but it will not last. Honey will revive you when you are hungry but you will need to eat again the next day. God's Word will give you strength for ever.

'By them is your servant warned; in keeping them there is great reward.' God's Law warns us about our own inadequacies and about the uncertainty of the future, in contrast to the security of keeping God's Law. It also promises us a great reward: eternal life with God. The Law is our teacher, showing us the way to God.

David starts by showing us that the sun, moon and stars can begin to point us to God. However, he warns us that if we stay there, our picture of God will be inadequate. We need to find God in his Word. Through studying the Word of God we can come to know the creator.

The only honest reaction as we encounter the creator in his Word is that of Isaiah: '"Woe to me!" I cried. "I am ruined! For I am a man of unclean lips, and I live among a people of unclean lips, and my eyes have seen the King, the Lord Almighty."' (Isaiah 6:5) There is no way that any human being can stand in the presence of the holy God.

This is where the Holy Spirit comes in. This is where we have to come to the cross and recognize that the only basis on which we can stand before God is by accepting that Jesus died for us. In humility, we ask for God's forgiveness.

The psalmist continues: 'Keep your servant also from wilful sins...' In another translation it says 'presumptuous sin'. When I was in a pantomime one year, I was greatly blessed because there were some Christians in the cast and other Christians in the company too. I got to know some of the other cast members quite well.

A group of us used to play trumps. It was £1 to play and I played and lost my money. One of the Christian dressers came in and said, 'Kriss, I am surprised at you, gambling.' I said, 'I am not gambling. I am paying to play.'

I did not care whether I won or lost and it was great fun. It passed the time and I saw it as paying to play, not gambling. The little group was made up of me, a Christian, another who was a noted philanderer and one of the others was an active homosexual. During the run of the show, I had opportunities to witness to each of them. They asked me about my faith. I was able to plant some seeds.

That young woman dresser presumed that she knew

me and that she knew my motivation. She presumed that she knew God's will for me.

Another time I was listening to a tape of the rock band, the Fugees, which belonged to my daughter. There were a couple of nice songs on it, which I really liked, but when I listened to the whole tape, I discovered that there was also some language on it that I could never use in a book like this!

Anyway, there I was listening to the tape and who should walk in but my dresser. As she came in, of course, we were at one of the places where the language was a bit tasty. She looked at me and said, 'Kriss, I am surprised at you!' She presumed that she knew what I was doing and that I was in the wrong. She had no idea that I was listening to my daughter's tape, partly to find out if it was suitable for her to have.

How we judge people may say more about ourselves than about the other person. We have a great habit of projecting our own sins on to other people. Have you ever noticed that sins look far worse when someone else is doing them than when we ourselves are doing them? There is also a danger in doing things that we presume are good and assuming that we will gain God's favour by doing them.

Let us finish this chapter by praying as David prayed. He said: 'May the words of my mouth and the meditation of my heart be pleasing in your sight, O Lord, my Rock and my Redeemer.'

Prayer

Lord, we want to be acceptable in your sight. We want our words to be your words. We want to be seasoned with your Word. We want to be seasoned with your presence. We want to know you in the power of your resurrection and the fellowship of your suffering. Father, we want to be what you want us to be, to be acceptable to you alone. Help us to be governed by your sun and not to run away to the darkness. May we turn towards you and allow the Holy Spirit to work in us. Amen

Psalm 22

For the director of music. To the tune of
'The Doe of the Morning'. A psalm of David.

My God, my God, why have you forsaken me?
  Why are you so far from saving me,
  so far from the words of my groaning?
O my God, I cry out by day, but you do not answer,
  by night, and am not silent.

Yet you are enthroned as the Holy One;
  you are the praise of Israel.
In you our fathers put their trust;
  they trusted and you delivered them.
They cried to you and were saved;
  in you they trusted and were not disappointed.

But I am a worm and not a man,
  scorned by men and despised by the people.
All who see me mock me;
  they hurl insults, shaking their heads:
'He trusts in the Lord;
  let the Lord rescue him.
Let him deliver him,
  since he delights in him.'

Yet you brought me out of the womb;
  you made me trust in you
  even at my mother's breast.
From birth I was cast upon you;
  from my mother's womb you have been my God.

Do not be far from me,
  for trouble is near
  and there is no one to help.

Many bulls surround me;
  strong bulls of Bashan encircle me.
Roaring lions tearing their prey
  open their mouths wide against me.
I am poured out like water,
  and all my bones are out of joint.
My heart has turned to wax;
  it has melted away within me.
My strength is dried up like a potsherd,
  and my tongue sticks to the roof of my mouth;
  you lay me in the dust of death.
Dogs have surrounded me;
  a band of evil men has encircled me,
  they have pierced my hands and my feet.
I can count all my bones;
  people stare and gloat over me.
They divide my garments among them
  and cast lots for my clothing.

But you, O Lord, be not far off;
  O my Strength, come quickly to help me.
Deliver my life from the sword,
  my precious life from the power of the dogs.
Rescue me from the mouth of the lions;
  save me from the horns of the wild oxen.

I will declare your name to my brothers;
  in the congregation I will praise you.
You who fear the Lord, praise him!
  All you descendants of Jacob, honour him!
  Revere him, all you descendants of Israel!

For he has not despised or disdained
  the suffering of the afflicted one;
he has not hidden his face from him
  but has listened to his cry for help.

From you comes the theme of my praise
  in the great assembly;
  before those who fear you will I fulfil my vows.
The poor will eat and be satisfied;
  they who seek the Lord will praise him—
  may your hearts live for ever!
All the ends of the earth
  will remember and turn to the Lord,
and all the families of the nations
  will bow down before him,
for dominion belongs to the Lord
  and he rules over the nations.

All the rich of the earth will feast and worship;
  all who go down to the dust will kneel before him—
  those who cannot keep themselves alive.
Posterity will serve him;
  future generations will be told about the Lord.
They will proclaim his righteousness
  to a people yet unborn—
  for he has done it.

This is a psalm which I like to read when things are not hunky-dory, when things are not cool running. If I were to try to categorize this psalm, I would put it down as a lament—but, of course, that is not a total description of the material contained within it.

While the content makes it a lament, Psalm 22 is probably best known because it was quoted by our Lord Jesus Christ on the cross, when he said, 'My God, my

God, why have you forsaken me?'

Evil is an ever-present reality in our lives. Pain and suffering are part and parcel of our lives. We can be sure that we will experience it in our lives at some time. When a catastrophe occurs, it is no consolation to those who experience it, but we must realize that pain and suffering are part of life. Evil cannot be explained without reference to the evil one.

The psalmist's opening statement is to ask God, 'why have you forsaken me?' In other words, where are you in my hour of need? He feels let down by God. Probably the worst pain a human being can experience is feeling cut off from God.

So many people in our society are dissatisfied with life and are looking for meaning in many different ways. Although they may not know it, they are crying out in a way similar to the psalmist: 'God where are you?'

From the beginning, Jesus had been with God. On the cross, for the first time, he experienced separation from God—for how long we do not know.

This was the psalmist's charge: 'Why are you so far from saving me, so far from the words of my groaning? O my God, I cry out by day, but you do not answer, by night, and am not silent.' The psalmist feels separated from God. It is the greatest pain that a human can suffer.

Suddenly his tone changes: 'Yet you are enthroned as the Holy One; you are the praise of Israel. In you our fathers put their trust; they trusted and you delivered them.'

He is saying, 'God, you are not there for me but I know you are holy.' The highest thing that you can say about God is that he is holy. As the songwriter puts it, he is a 'God of faithfulness, without injustice…'

Although the psalmist feels let down by God, he

clings to the historical faith that he has been taught as a boy: 'in you our fathers put their trust...' He goes further in expressing to God not only the fact that his forefathers had trusted in God but that they had found God faithful. He expresses the same thought three times: '...they trusted and you delivered them. They cried to you and were saved; in you they trusted and were not disappointed.'

The cry of the psalmist's heart is this: 'In the past, God, the people trusted you and you acted to save them. How come in my hour of need, I can't say the same? I have read all these things. People have told me of God's faithfulness but it is not my experience.'

I am sure that there are people reading this book who feel exactly that. You go to church, sing all those wonderful hymns about what God has done, you hear people from the front sharing their experience but deep in your heart you can't help thinking, 'OK, but that is not my experience when I have problems.'

The psalmist is being real. He does not want any façade here. He is saying, 'Lord, I have heard all these things. I know all the right answers, but in my hour of need I am hurting and you are not there.'

'But I am a worm and not a man, scorned by men and despised by the people. All who see me mock me; they hurl insults, shaking their heads:'

The psalmist is suffering social pain. He feels excluded, ostracized. He feels that he does not fit into society. He feels that people are laughing at him.

I know a bit about this myself. As I was growing up, things were not as politically correct as they are now. I used to get all the racial abuse at school—sambo, nignog, coon and so on. I used to have a few fisticuffs to explain my position!

When I became an adult, I thought I had left all those things behind me. Recently, however, I went to a football match at Portsmouth. After the game I was walking down the road and there was a crowd of kids who recognized me and wanted to have my hat as a souvenir. Then, all of a sudden, a guy on the other side of the road shouted across, 'Look who it is, that black *****!'

I am Christian; I am supposed to turn the other cheek and so on. But in that moment I put down my bags, walked across the road and said to that guy, 'You are not being funny.' I thought about punching him. In the end, some people around said, 'Leave him, Kriss. He is not worth it.' They pulled him away and I walked off.

I reacted to it because it made me feel social pain. I was born in this country, but I don't consider myself English. Being English is about being white. As I was growing up, I was told I wasn't English because I was black. The chap at Portsmouth felt that I could not be a Pompey (Portsmouth FC) supporter because I was black.

The psalmist not only has spiritual pain—because he feels that God has left him—he also feels social pain, that he has been excluded by his fellow countrymen. He is despised by the people. They mock him and laugh at him.

The psalmist's predicament gets worse. The people are now telling him that God does not love him any more. He trusts in the Lord; let the Lord rescue him. Let him deliver him. The implication of what they are saying is: if he was a good man, God would help him. As God isn't helping him, then he cannot be a good man.

It is the same situation that we find ourselves in when we are telling someone about God and then we lose our job, or our car gets stolen, and our friend says, 'Great God you've got, who lets all this happen to you! If that is your Christianity, you can keep it.'

The psalmist moves on in his thinking. 'Yet you brought me out of the womb; you made me trust in you even at my mother's breast.' What the psalmist is saying here is that there was a time when he was even more vulnerable than he is now—when he was a newborn baby.

He recalls that God looked after him in those days. 'From birth I was cast upon you; from my mother's womb you have been my God.' He is now asking, 'God, if you were there for me when I was first born, please be there for me again now.'

His plea to God is: Do not be far from me, for trouble is near and there is no one to help. I know that you have done great things for Israel. I know that you have looked after me in the past. Will you be there for me again now?

The psalmist uses graphic language to describe his plight: 'Many bulls surround me; strong bulls of Bashan encircle me. Roaring lions tearing their prey open their mouths wide against me.' Do you think that he might be feeling a little scared, perhaps? He is saying that in his moment of weakness, everyone seems extra big, extra aggressive, and they are ready to rip his head off! They are ready to sort him out.

'I am poured out like water, and all my bones are out of joint. My heart has turned to wax; it has melted away within me. My strength is dried up like a potsherd, and my tongue sticks to the roof of my mouth…' This is great poetry. He is on his last legs. He is really suffering. He feels in such a state that he is good for nothing. This is ultimate physical pain.

But the physical pain is compounded by the social pain: 'Dogs have surrounded me; a band of evil men has encircled me' and there is also the psychological suffering of having his clothes ripped off his back.

He trusted in God, but God does not seem to be there. He trusted in his friends He has trusted in his body—perhaps he was an athlete—but now his strength is not there any more. Even the psychological comfort of his clothes has been taken away. He is experiencing being totally alone and totally humiliated.

But even in the midst of his difficulties he utters the words 'Rescue me… save me!' This is the psalmist's prayer: Save me! Save me! Save me! Save me!

The tone changes in verse 24: '…he has not hidden his face from him but has listened to his cry for help.' Imagine the relief and joy that the psalmist felt. He had finally got through to God and God listened. Imagine what it would be like for you. One thing this psalm teaches me is always to have hope.

No matter what your problems, no matter what you're suffering—even if you are going through a period of spiritual dryness, where the Bible does not seem to make sense, if your prayer life is like a desert, if you suffer illness or have problems at work—do not give up hope. Where there is faith, there is hope.

In the end the psalmist could say, 'What I have been told, what I have read in the scriptures is true. I know it is true because I have experienced it. I was in trouble and God heard me and answered.' Where there was faith there is now hope and salvation.

The psalmist was aware of what God had done for Israel at so many times in its history, yet when he needed God, where was he? He was so upset. He was lost. Then God answered and his response was: 'I will declare your name to my brothers; in the congregation I will praise you.'

When we go through difficult times we begin to understand other people better. As we suffer we can empathize better with other people who are suffering.

The psalmist can now stand up in the congregation and declare that God had not forsaken him. In verse 4, the psalmist had said: 'In you our fathers put their trust; they trusted and you delivered them.' Now he expresses the same thought—but this time it is from conviction, from his own experience.

He says, 'I was in trouble; I was in despair. I was down in the dumps. No one was there for me but guess what—it was all right on the night! It turned round, because God was there for me. In my moment of need, God heard and answered.'

Sometimes we go through hard times so that afterwards we can sympathize with other people and help them, so that we can stand up in church and share with people how God has brought us through the crisis.

We live in a society where we don't want to grow old. Look at me: I am almost forty and I still wear a baseball cap back to front! Women in their thirties and forties dress like their daughters. So the daughters have to wear more and more outrageous clothes to avoid looking like their mothers!

We are a society that wants to do it our way. We do not want to have role models, or to listen to the wisdom of someone who has lived longer than we have. But we need to.

Our society has lost the respect for the wisdom of older generations which the ancient world had. We are not interested in hearing older people standing up and saying, 'I have been there and this is my experience.' In our society, it is much more the case that young people say, 'You are out of touch. Your views are irrelevant and old-fashioned.'

But we can learn so much from listening to older

people who can stand up and say, 'I have walked with the Lord for over fifty years and this is my experience. I have had problems but this is how the Lord has led me through.'

The psalmist's testimony was, 'Don't worry because God was there for me in the end. You can have faith in him that he will be there for you too.' The difference was that in his society the people were willing to listen to him.

When we are in trouble we tend to pray, 'Lord, if you get me out of this mess, then I will do anything you want me to!' I remember getting a hamstring injury shortly before the 1988 Olympics. I just prayed, 'Lord, if you let me run in the Olympics I will tell everyone about you.' I was singing inside as I ran round that Olympic track. I was saying, 'Look what God did to me, how he healed my hamstring!'

When God works in our lives, we need to be ready to stand up before the whole congregation and tell people what he has done, so that our people can learn from and be encouraged by our experience.

Suffering and difficulties are a certainty in life. Sometimes they happen randomly. Other times we can see them coming. We need to understand this, to be ready, to be prepared and most of all to understand that with God there is light at the end of the tunnel. The testimony of others who have already gone through this can help us to face our trials with confidence.

When you are going through your pain, people are watching; unbelievers are watching how you cope and whether this God that you believe in will do anything for you. The psalmist says: 'All the ends of the earth will remember and turn to the Lord.' It is as if he is holding up a great banner so that people can see who God is and what he has done. When they hear your testimony they might even turn towards God.

The word 'remember' interests me. It suggests that they used to believe and that they just need to be reminded. It is one of my theories that people have to learn to be atheists. Most people start off with a belief in God—OK, they may not know who they believe in—but they start off with a belief in a greater being, but then education (so-called), peer pressure, evil desire, and so on, dissuade them (see the parable of the sower in Matthew 13).

'...and all the families of the nations will bow down before him, for dominion belongs to the Lord and he rules over the nations.' A day is coming when everyone will bow down before God. As Paul writes in Philippians, '...at the name of Jesus every knee should bow, in heaven and on earth and under the earth.' (Philippians 2:10) Oh how much better to do it willingly and voluntarily!

Not only will the congregation worship the God they had heard about in nursery rhymes, there is more. They will proclaim his righteousness to a people yet unborn—for he has done it.

The 'pièce de resistance' is this: those who are yet to come will worship God because of the psalmist. This has been fulfilled. We are the living proof of this as we use Psalm 22 in our worship. Our righteous walk with God can lead future generations to follow God.

Pain and suffering is a reality in life but I believe that God feels it with us. Sometimes we cannot see God or experience his presence at the time but as we look back, we can see where he has been with us.

I want to finish with five points about suffering:

1. It produces fruit. Think about your own salvation that was won by Jesus' suffering. Jesus did not come to drive a series 3 BMW. Jesus did not come to have a credit card. Jesus did not come to be a popular celebrity. Jesus came to seek and to save the lost, to suffer and to pay the price.

    The church grew through the suffering and martyrdom of Stephen. I believe, too, that when we come through suffering and difficult experiences we silence the devil—think of the story of Job. In Philippians 3:10 Paul says: 'I want to know Christ and the power of his resurrection and the fellowship of sharing in his sufferings, becoming like him in his death.' Suffering will make us more like Jesus.

2. Suffering teaches us dependence. It teaches us that we haven't all the answers, that we cannot do it alone. It teaches us to depend on God.

3. Suffering refines us. Sometimes we suffer as a result of our own sin and folly. Often God uses suffering to bring good out of a difficult situation.

4. Suffering can be a rebuke, a discipline from God. It can be God's way of bringing us back into line with his will.

5. Suffering can increase our ministry. It has been said that you cannot see the picture unless you are inside the frame. Having experienced suffering can help you to get alongside someone else who is going through the same experience.

Prayer

Father, we thank you so much for our faith; that can be such a help to us in times of trouble. You are a strong tower and the righteous run into you and are safe. Lord we can be knocked from pillar to post. We see evil all around us. We cannot comprehend everything that goes on about us. Sometimes we feel dried up as we walk with you, but we know that we can look to you as the author and finisher of our faith. We have this hope, Lord, that you will be with us in our time of need. Amen

Psalm 34

Of David. When he pretended to be insane before
Abimelech, who drove him away, and he left.

I will extol the Lord at all times;
* his praise will always be on my lips.*
My soul will boast in the Lord;
* let the afflicted hear and rejoice.*
Glorify the Lord with me;
* let us exalt his name together.*

I sought the Lord, and he answered me;
* he delivered me from all my fears.*
Those who look to him are radiant;
* their faces are never covered with shame.*
This poor man called, and the Lord heard him;
* he saved him out of all his troubles.*
The angel of the Lord encamps
*   around those who fear him,*
* and he delivers them.*

Taste and see that the Lord is good;
* blessed is the man who takes refuge in him.*
Fear the Lord, you his saints,
* for those who fear him lack nothing.*
The lions may grow weak and hungry,
* but those who seek the Lord lack no good thing.*

Come, my children, listen to me;
* I will teach you the fear of the Lord.*
Whoever of you loves life and
* desires to see many good days,*

keep your tongue from evil
and your lips from speaking lies.
Turn from evil and do good;
seek peace and pursue it.

The eyes of the Lord are on the righteous
and his ears are attentive to their cry;
the face of the Lord is against those who do evil,
to cut off the memory of them from the earth.

The righteous cry out, and the Lord hears them;
he delivers them from all their troubles.
The Lord is close to the broken-hearted
and saves those who are crushed in spirit.

A righteous man may have many troubles,
but the Lord delivers him from them all;
he protects all his bones,
not one of them will be broken.

Evil will slay the wicked;
the foes of the righteous will be condemned.
The Lord redeems his servants;
no-one will be condemned who takes refuge in him.

Psalm 34 is a declarative psalm, one which declares what God has done in someone's life. I believe that it would be helpful for each of us to have such a psalm of our own, declaring what God has done in our life.

The psalm begins with a clear declaration: 'I will extol the Lord at all times...' Not sometimes, not even most of the time, but at all times. Not just on Sunday mornings, but all through the week too.

'His praise will always be on my lips.' Paul writes in Romans chapter 10 verse 9: '…if you confess with your mouth, "Jesus is Lord," and believe in your heart that God raised him from the dead, you will be saved.'

'My soul will boast in the Lord…' I find this verse very interesting. Being in the media, and in the motivational business, I am working in an environment where it is the norm to be very self-assertive, very self-confident. To know what you can do and make sure that others know it too. By contrast, the psalmist says that our only boasting should be in the Lord.

The psalmist begins by setting out his stall—he is going to extol the Lord at all times. Now he invites others to join him: 'Glorify the Lord with me; let us exalt his name together.'

The motto on my school blazer was *Non Nobis Solum*. I wore it for years without knowing what it meant and then I found out—'not for us alone'. That is what the psalmist is saying. Our experience of God is not for us alone. It is something that we are to share with others.

Why does the psalmist want to praise God at all times? What is motivating him to extol the Lord at all times? It is his experience of God. The next four verses give us details of the experiences that he has had which have motivated him to praise God. The clear message of this psalm is that when he was in trouble, God heard and answered.

There was a guy in the Bible called Ishmael and in fact the name Ishmael means, 'God heard'. This psalmist would have been happy to have been called Ishmael, for he believed that God heard.

I do not know why it is that we go through troubles, but rest assured of this: when we do, God hears. He hears when we cry out in trouble. As the psalmist says, 'I sought the Lord, and he answered me; he delivered me from all my fears.'

When I became a Christian in 1987 I was in the army. I was at a stage in my athletics where my career was about to take off. From the point of view of my athletics it was time to go full time but the question in my mind was this: if I gave up the security of a regular army pay packet, how would I feed my wife and daughter?

God answered. He took away my fears and assured me that he would look after me. This does not mean that we should jump off a cliff and challenge God to look after us. But if God speaks into your life and calls you to do something, you can be sure that he will take care of all your needs.

The psalmist says, '…he delivered me from all my fears.' What are our fears? What worries you? The psalmist had lots of troubles, lots of fears, but when he called to God he was delivered. We do not get any time-frame here. Did God hear him on the first day, in the first week, or in the first year? What we do know is that God heard him.

As a kid, I lived in a children's home. Everywhere I went I would hear people say, 'That's the poor kid from the children's home.' But when I look back now I can see God working in my life, drawing me out of that unpromising situation to where I am now. God had his hand on my life, even when I did not know him.

As I look back on my life, I don't know why a lot of things happened. I don't know why I had to grow up in a children's home, wondering every day if my mother and father were going to come and pick me up. But I do know this, that God worked miracles in my life.

I know he heard me when, as a little boy, I lay in bed

crying for my mum. When I saw other boys and girls going home to their parents and wondered when it was going to be my turn. Then, as I reached the age of sixteen, I realized that it was never going to be my turn. I can thank God that he was with me and brought me through. The experiences stood me in good stead.

I don't know what experiences you are going through at the moment, or why you are going through them, but maybe it is so that you can say, with the psalmist, 'I sought the Lord, and he answered me; he delivered me from all my fears...' and that you can be a witness to other people.

Think what it would be like if Christians never had any problems. Could we really relate to the world? Could we really come alongside other people? Could we help other people who are hurting? Could we be there for them?

I don't know what the psalmist's problem was, but I do know this, that in his hour of need he was able to say, 'I sought the Lord, and he answered me; he delivered me from all my fears...'

We are not alone; we can look through the annals of history and say, with the writer to the Hebrews, '...we are surrounded by such a great cloud of witnesses...' (Hebrews 12:1).

The psalmist identifies himself with some of these people: 'Those who look to him are radiant; their faces are never covered with shame. This poor man called, and the Lord heard him; he saved him out of all his troubles. The angel of the Lord encamps around those who fear him, and he delivers them.' He is saying, in effect, 'If you don't believe me, ask some of the others who have experienced God in their life and they will give you the same answer.' He says that it is not just his experience, that there are many who have experienced God's help in their lives.

Whatever your beliefs, when you fail to live up to the standards you have set yourself, there is guilt and shame. The worst nightmare is to encounter someone who has no shame or guilt, someone with a weapon who will blow your brains out because he has no guilt, no sense that what he is doing is wrong.

We live in a society which tries to get rid of shame. We say, 'Each to his own,' or 'Live and let live.' Society has rejected absolutes. When we Christians say that there are moral absolutes, God's revealed standards, we make ourselves unpopular.

Shame comes when there is a moral code that all of society accepts. The psalmist could say this because his people all owed allegiance to the God of Israel and adhered to the covenant of Sinai. They could say that if you were outside that framework, you were shameful.

'Those who look to him are radiant; their faces are never covered with shame.' Even when the people sinned, if they turned from their sin and back to God, recognizing that he was their God, they had no longer any cause to be ashamed.

It is my experience, with the psalmist, that 'This poor man called, and the Lord heard him; he saved him out of all his troubles.' How does God save us from troubles? As we have seen already, troubles surely come, even to Christians. But when these troubles come, God will pull us through and give us people to help us. I have proved that to be true in my own life. I can say with the psalmist: 'The angel of the Lord encamps around those who fear him, and he delivers them.' Having talked about his experience, having told his story, having said, 'this has been my experience,' he makes it personal and throws out a challenge to the people to check it out for themselves: 'Taste and see that the Lord is good…' 'You can have this, too,' he says!

I remember how, when my daughter was very small, she would be offered something new to eat, and would often react, 'Don't like it, don't like it!' I would protest, 'But you have never had it before.' She would continue, 'Don't like it, don't like it!' She had already made up her mind, even before tasting it.

There are many people like that in our society. They don't know the Bible, or anything about Christianity. They have no grasp of the basics. Yet those same people will say about Christianity, 'Don't like it, don't like it!' The truth is that they have absolutely no grasp of what it is they don't like!

Once, when I was speaking in a university, a student came up to me afterwards and said, 'Kriss, that is just your experience. It doesn't make it true just because it is your experience. I like the way I am living my life and I don't need you to tell me how I should lead my life.'

I said, 'I agree. You should not believe it just because it is my experience. But, tell me this, how are you going to know if it is any good unless you look into it, read the Bible and see what it says?' He had never read the Bible, but he had already made up his mind that Christianity was rubbish. The psalmist said to the people, 'Taste and see that the Lord is good…' Check it out and find out for yourselves that it is true.

'Whoever of you loves life and desires to see many good days, keep your tongue from evil and your lips from speaking lies.' Recently, I found myself with a group of TV people. We were sitting around, talking and laughing. Some of the jokes were a bit naughty, but they were funny!

I started to join in and I told one. Everyone was laughing. Then one person said, 'Kriss, I thought you were a Christian.' When he said that I realized that my mouth was not pure. I was sending conflicting messages. On the one hand, I was standing for God; on the other I was telling stories full of *double entendre* and sexual innuendo.

The psalmist's message is simple: be careful of your tongue or it will get you into trouble. The tension for us is that as people we want to be seen as hip and happening. We don't want to come across as nerds. We want to be there when the jokes are rolling. We want to be part of it—and there is nothing wrong in any of this. Yet the psalmist reminds us that what we say creates a reality around us.

But what do we do? We come to church on a Sunday, for an hour. If we are really rolling, we have our ten minutes of quiet time each day. And if we are really getting the points, we do a little prayer at bedtime. That adds up to a maximum of three hours per week. What happens to the rest of the week?

We spend so much of the rest of our time watching TV. What is your speech pattern creating? What is the major influence on your life? Is it the Spirit of God, or the world? What comes in through your eyes and ears, creates your reality and then goes out again through your mouth.

The psalmist says: 'Whoever of you loves life and desires to see many good days, keep your tongue from evil and your lips from speaking lies.' We all do it—deception, speaking false words, speaking with forked tongue, saying one thing but meaning another. Once you start saying it, you can bet your bottom dollar that before long you will be doing it too.

Take a verse like Romans chapter 10 verse 9: '...If

you confess with your mouth, "Jesus is Lord," and believe in your heart that God raised him from the dead, you will be saved.'

Why do you think it says to 'confess with your mouth'? Because when you have told someone, then you are on your way. It has become part of your life.

'Turn from evil and do good; seek peace and pursue it.' The eyes of the Lord are on the righteous and his ears are attentive to their cry; When I read this, I thought about my dog. When I have been away for a week, my dog is always ready to greet me. Recently, when I had just come home, he was in my Range Rover, which was parked on our driveway, and he saw me. He was trying to break the glass, to beat his way out of the car to get to me. He really wanted to get to see me fast. Now I am not, for one moment, saying that there is a connection between God and my dog (even though the word God is dog backwards)!

But, in that moment, my dog was attentive to my cry and the psalmist tells us that God is attentive to our cries. He wants to help us. God can't wait for us to call to him. He wants to hear and help us. As we pray and read the Bible, God is waiting to meet us.

Can you see how this whole psalm is about speaking? The whole psalm is about the power of the word. When you call to God with righteousness and an open heart, he listens.

'The face of the Lord is against those who do evil, to cut off the memory of them from the earth.' This verse is not for those who love him, but for those who do not; he has turned his back on them. Look at Isaiah chapter 59 verse 2: 'But your iniquities have separated you from your God; your sins have hidden his face from you, so that he will not hear.'

What this is saying is that there comes a point when God turns his back and leaves us to it. I know that the times when I get into difficulty are times when I hear God's voice and don't listen to it. But, after a bit, we no longer even hear God speaking to us.

Often we make the mistake of thinking, 'I know where I have to draw the line. I can go to that point but not step over it.' The problem is that we go right up to the edge, not realizing that it is like a vortex, which sucks us in and over the line. When you start setting limits and think, 'I can do this but if I do that, I come off the pace', you have been sucked into the devil's lair.

If I am not going to fall into sexual sin, I know that I must avoid going to certain parties. I know that I must not do that or there is the danger that I will be sucked in.

There is nothing wrong with parties, beer, or the opposite sex. A social life is part of God's creation. But I know from experience that if I put myself in certain situations I can easily be sucked into the vortex. The party is innocent enough, but I know where it can lead to. In those situations we need to listen to the Spirit's leading. Often we need to hear the Spirit before we get into the party, or the music will be so loud that we will no longer be able to hear him. You need to know where your own problem areas are.

'The righteous cry out, and the Lord hears them; he delivers them from all their troubles. The Lord is close to the broken-hearted and saves those who are crushed in spirit.'

We have to confess our sin. 'God, I have messed up again. I know that I cannot live according to the Law. I cannot live without you.' When we follow God's Spirit, we do not need to worry about laws. You will struggle, stumble and fall but the more you listen to the Spirit, the more you will be able to follow in God's way.

'He delivers them…' Think about times in your own life when things seemed impossible and God delivered you. As you look back, perhaps you can think of some situations where you felt a barrier was so great that you would never be able to get over it.

The picture here is of someone on their deathbed, fighting to get out of the body, knowing that death would be a release from all the troubles. In your life, you can expect to have trouble but—be sure of this—God will lead you through it.

The psalmist wants you to have an experience of God and to be liberated through it.

Prayer

Father, can we really hold to that promise that we will lack nothing? Show us and guide us, Lord. We want to be people whose faith has endured. Father, we look forward to the day when we will be with you. We know that we will face trials and tests. Help us to endure to the end. Help us to see you as the author and finisher of our faith. Help us to set our eyes on Jesus and to have heaven as our goal. By your Spirit, enlighten us and continue to speak to us. Help us to flee from the devil and listen to the still small voice of God. Help us to endure temptation and come out the other side. In your matchless name we pray. Amen

Psalm 40

For the director of music. Of David. A psalm.

I waited patiently for the Lord;
he turned to me and heard my cry.
He lifted me out of the slimy pit,
out of the mud and mire;
he set my feet on a rock
and gave me a firm place to stand.
He put a new song in my mouth,
a hymn of praise to our God.
Many will see and fear
and put their trust in the Lord.

Blessed is the man
who makes the Lord his trust,
who does not look to the proud,
to those who turn aside to false gods.
Many, O Lord my God,
are the wonders you have done.
The things you planned for us
no one can recount to you;
were I to speak and tell of them,
they would be too many to declare.

Sacrifice and offering you did not desire,
but my ears you have pierced;
burnt offerings and sin offerings
you did not require.
Then I said, 'Here I am, I have come—
it is written about me in the scroll.

I desire to do your will, O my God;
  your law is within my heart.'

I proclaim righteousness in the great assembly;
  I do not seal my lips,
  as you know, O Lord.
I do not hide your righteousness in my heart;
  I speak of your faithfulness and salvation.
I do not conceal your love and your truth
  from the great assembly.

Do not withhold your mercy from me, O Lord;
  may your love and your truth always protect me.
For troubles without number surround me;
  my sins have overtaken me, and I cannot see.
They are more than the hairs of my head,
  and my heart fails within me.

Be pleased, O Lord, to save me;
  O Lord, come quickly to help me.
May all who seek to take my life
  be put to shame and confusion;
may all who desire my ruin
  be turned back in disgrace.
May those who say to me, 'Aha! Aha!'
  be appalled at their own shame.
But may all who seek you
  rejoice and be glad in you;
may those who love your salvation always say,
  'The Lord be exalted!'

Yet I am poor and needy;
  may the Lord think of me.
You are my help and my deliverer;
  O my God, do not delay.

This is a Messianic psalm. Even though it was written 500 or 600 years before Christ, some of the psalm has to do with Christ. I love it when I find a passage in the Old Testament which confirms some New Testament event, because in that way scripture verifies Christ's ministry. It heralds Christ and is a testimony to him before he even came. Likewise, Christ, in fulfilling the scriptures, verifies them and says, 'Yes, these scriptures speak of me.'

Psalm 40 is one of the many psalms attributed to David. It is a petition; it is a lament; it is a cry from his heart. He starts off with a statement: 'I waited patiently for the Lord…' What was he waiting for? How long did he wait? What was his time-frame? It is much easier to wait if you know how long you will be waiting—like when you see a notice, 'Back in five minutes.'

We have no idea how long the psalmist had to wait. From the way he says that he waited with patience, we may guess that he waited a long time.

Think for a moment about some of the early experiences of David's life. As the youngest of the family, he was used to being mocked by his brothers. Even when he came into Saul's court, Saul used to take the mickey out of him. Ultimately, Saul became very jealous of David and pursued him. David was used to being in situations where he was an outcast. David had many opportunities to learn patience.

Even when he became king, there are unpleasant incidents in his life—like the one where his wife Michal laughed at him when he was singing and dancing and praising God. David was accustomed to being put down. But in all these experiences, perhaps David learned to be patient and to trust in God.

David also learned that God was with him in all the difficult situations that he faced. Although his brothers laughed at him, in God's strength he went out and killed Goliath. He waited his turn, waited for God's time and ultimately became the greatest king that Israel ever had.

David knew from experience that if he waited patiently God would hear and answer. Remember what Paul writes to the Romans: 'Not only so, but we also rejoice in our sufferings, because we know that suffering produces perseverance; perseverance, character; and character, hope. And hope does not disappoint us, because God has poured out his love into our hearts by the Holy Spirit, whom he has given us.' (Romans 5:3–5)

David had confidence because of the experiences in his life. He had learned to wait for God and knew that God would hear. He did not need to know if it would be five minutes, one day or one year. He knew that if he waited, God would respond.

That was indeed the outcome: '…he turned to me and heard my cry.' Then, as we continue, there is a three-point sermon waiting to be preached from verse 2:

▶ *'He lifted me out of the slimy pit…'*

▶ *'…he set my feet on a rock…'*

▶ *'…and gave me a firm place to stand.'*

God brought him up out of a horrible place. The idea David is trying to convey is that whatever he was going through in his life, it was like falling into a deep pit and being unable to get out. Every way he tried, his feet were slipping and sliding around. It was a place from which he could not extricate himself.

God heard him and lifted him up out of it and put

him on a stable place from where he could move on. Perhaps you have had an experience where everything seemed to be against you, where your back was against the wall, where you couldn't get out. Wait patiently for God and he will rescue you and establish you on a rock.

God takes us from our sins, establishes us in Christ and then starts to move us forward. Here, David is beginning to move forward. We may make plans but it is God who establishes our ways.

'He put a new song in my mouth, a hymn of praise…' Originally, the psalmist was sad and crying, but now he has a new song in his heart. It is a song of praise to God. His sorrow has turned to singing, his mourning to dancing.

The outcome is: 'Many will see and fear and put their trust in the Lord.' When we go through trials and difficulties, we are prone to ask, 'Why me? For I have done nothing.' As he looked back at the hard times, David was able to see that through watching his experience, many people praised God and put their trust in him.

Sometimes we go through hard times, not just for our own good but for those who are around us, that they can learn from what we have gone through. As those around see how you deal with your suffering, the way you cope when your back is against the wall and how God lifts you up, they see and praise and put their trust in the Lord.

We are not trusting in lies; our trust is in God. David did not put his faith in people. He did not trust in human ideas; his faith was in God. He knew God personally. He knew God was there in his time of need. He had the evidence. 'The things you planned for us no one can recount to you; were I to speak and tell of them, they would be too many to declare.'

David knew a personal God and he knew that he could wait for God and that God would hear and act.

In verses 6–10 we come to the Messianic part of the psalm. 'Sacrifice and offering you did not desire, but my ears you have pierced; burnt offerings and sin offerings you did not require.'

This verse is, at first glance, quite hard to understand because in the Old Testament, sacrifice and offering were precisely what God did require! It makes a nonsense of Leviticus if indeed sacrifice and offering are not required. Had Israel got it wrong all those years?

The answer is that David is beginning to speak in a prophetic spirit. The first five verses have been describing the past. Now we move on to the future. David looks to the future and sees a time when the sacrifice system has been overtaken by the death of Jesus. David is expressing something that he could never have understood if it had not been revealed to him by God.

Remember John's vision in Revelation 21 of the New Jerusalem: 'I did not see a temple in the city, because the Lord God Almighty and the Lamb are its temple.' (Revelation 21:22)

There was no need for a temple or for sacrifices because Jesus was the ultimate sacrifice. What he did at Calvary could not have been accomplished by anyone else or in any other way. We can look back and see that it has happened in history; David could only look forward in hope. We need to long for the New Jerusalem, where there will be no sin any more.

'I do not conceal your love and your truth from the great assembly.' When I was a kid, I was a real expert at hiding my sweets in my pocket and getting the paper off, in my pocket, so that no one would know that I had sweets and I would not have to share them with anyone.

God is not like that. God has good news and he has revealed it to everyone. Each of us can be part of it.

The next bit is amazing, when we remember how the psalm started with David waiting patiently, and how it continued with him looking forward to the future. Now we find him saying: 'Do not withhold your mercy from me, O Lord; may your love and your truth always protect me.'

David is now ready to praise God, even when he is going through hard times. In verse 5 he was saying: 'The things you planned for us no one can recount to you…' Now he is concerned that troubles without number surround him. It is all a matter of perspective.

When he looks at God, he sees all the good things that God does in his life, and then he can glorify God. However, when he looks at himself and sees all the bad things which are happening, it gets him down.

Sometimes, we are asked to declare the good things that God has done and we find it hard. We would find it easier to list all the bad things that are going on in our lives. That sums up where we are.

When David was focusing on God, he could write beautiful psalms about what God was doing in his life, but when David's heart was turned towards himself, he would be writing about the evil things that were going on in his life. Here he is now, admitting that things are overwhelming him, that he is back in the dark, deep pit of despair with no way out. He sees his sins so clearly.

All of us who are Christians know that God has taken away our sins, but at times we can be trapped by them and Satan can remind us of them. The psalmist says that his sins '…are more than the hairs of my head…' If that is so, perhaps I am luckier than some of you!

This is what David is waiting patiently for. His prayer

is: 'Be pleased, O Lord, to save me; O Lord, come quickly to help me.' If you are anxious about something, talk to God about it. Of course, God knows about it already—but it may help to know that you have told him about it.

Then David prays: 'May all who seek to take my life be put to shame and confusion; may all who desire my ruin be turned back in disgrace. May those who say to me, 'Aha! Aha!' be appalled at their own shame.' His prayer is that the proud and those who are against him be brought to shame, that those who taunt him will get their comeuppance.

Can you pray with the psalmist, '...may those who love your salvation always say, "The Lord be exalted!"', even when everything is going badly? He has seen what the future has in store, but back in the present he is feeling poor and needy. Despite that, he knows that God has not forgotten him and that God will act to save him. David put his faith in God and he was not disappointed.

Prayer

Help us, Lord, to wait patiently for you. We live in a world where everything is 'Now' and we expect instant answers. Teach us to put our trust in you and to wait patiently, believing that you will answer in your own time. For you, O Lord, are our help and our deliverer. Amen

Psalm 46

For the director of music. Of the Sons of Korah.
According to *alamoth*. A song.

God is our refuge and strength,
  an ever-present help in trouble.
Therefore we will not fear, though the earth give way
  and the mountains fall into the heart of the sea,
though its waters roar and foam
  and the mountains quake with their surging. Selah

There is a river whose streams make glad the city of God,
  the holy place where the Most High dwells.
God is within her, she will not fall;
  God will help her at break of day.
Nations are in uproar, kingdoms fall;
  he lifts his voice, the earth melts.

The Lord Almighty is with us;
  the God of Jacob is our fortress. Selah

Come and see the works of the Lord,
  the desolations he has brought on the earth.
He makes wars cease to the ends of the earth;
  he breaks the bow and shatters the spear,
  he burns the shields with fire.
'Be still, and know that I am God;
  I will be exalted among the nations,
  I will be exalted in the earth.'

The Lord Almighty is with us;
  the God of Jacob is our fortress. Selah

As I read this psalm, it seemed to me that there were two important issues. The psalm has to do with the end times. While the psalm certainly had a meaning for the writer in his own time, it also has for us, ultimately, a meaning in the times still to come. It is an apocalyptic psalm.

'God is our refuge and strength, an ever-present help in trouble.' The first two words of the psalm are 'God is'. The writer knew that God was there. Many clever people in our generation would question that. They are not convinced that God exists. The psalmist was convinced.

Many words can be added to those two words. God is *love*; God is *holy*; God is *near*; God is *our refuge and strength*. All of that, however, is meaningless without the knowledge that 'God is'.

'God is our refuge…' Refuge is a sanctuary, a hiding-place, somewhere to go in times of trouble. God is all that to us. God is also our 'strength', our power in moments of weakness. Remember what Paul wrote: 'My grace is sufficient for you, for my power is made perfect in weakness.' (2 Corinthians 12:9)

In moments of weakness we need a refuge and God is that refuge. God is our order in a sea of troubles, 'an ever-present help in trouble'. To help means to be alongside someone, to aid, to be of service, to enable someone to do something that they otherwise could not do on their own. The psalmist knew that God was the people's help, their refuge, their strength, that he was there for them in times of trouble.

If that is the case, there was no reason to fear. Fear is the opposite of faith. The people knew that God is. If they knew that, then there was never any need for them to fear. The Israelites knew all about trouble. They had

had trouble in Egypt. They had had trouble coming out of Egypt. God had set them free. Through those days, God was with them. They learned about faith in those days.

Faith is our ability to believe in God and see his perspective, whatever our circumstances and in spite of appearances. Our ability to trust God is directly related to our knowledge of God. These guys knew God as their 'refuge and strength' when they were confronted with trouble. Their faith in God, despite appearances, was what sustained them.

Israel was a sea-bordered country and a mountainous country, so the idea that 'the mountains fall into the heart of the sea' was something that they could understand. For the Israelites, too, the mountains were spiritual places—where Moses received the Ten Commandments, where Elijah took on the prophets of Baal. The sea was for the ancient people a place of foreboding. What the psalmist was saying, in the language of his people, was that even if the powers of evil were to prevail over the holy places in Israel, they need not fear, for God is their refuge and strength.

What could happen in our day? If there was a financial collapse or political uprising, how would that affect us? Would that shake us? Would we be able, in such a crisis, to say: 'God is our refuge and strength, an ever-present help in trouble'?

'There is a river whose streams make glad the city of God, the holy place where the Most High dwells.' This reminds me of Revelation chapter 22 verses 1–5: 'Then the angel showed me the river of the water of life, as clear as crystal, flowing from the throne of God and of the Lamb down the middle of the great street of the city. On each side of the river stood the tree of life, bearing twelve crops of fruit, yielding its fruit every month. And the leaves of the tree are for the healing of the nations. No longer will there be any curse. The throne of God and of the Lamb will be in the city, and his servants will serve him. They will see his face, and his name will be on their foreheads. There will be no more night. They will not need the light of a lamp or the light of the sun, for the Lord God will give them light. And they will reign for ever and ever.'

The 'city of God' is the dwelling place of God.

The reference to God as 'the Most High' may not mean much to us but remember the pluralistic context in which this psalm was written. It meant that God was greater than Osiris, the Egyptian God, greater than Baal, the Canaanite God. The psalmist was issuing a challenge to the nations: name your god, but I guarantee that ours is higher.

'Nations are in uproar, kingdoms fall; he lifts his voice, the earth melts.' This is a very important verse for our times. The nations and kingdoms are in uproar. My reading of the Bible tells me that there is coming a day when there will be one political leader, one economic system, one world religion.

When the psalmist was writing, satellites and computers were, of course, unheard of. Now, in our day, we can see more clearly how easy it would be for this to happen. I believe that the day is coming when the nations will rise up against Israel; that the tiny land of Israel will be the centre of world attention. When these events happen, we should see them in the context of what the psalmist and other biblical writers are saying.

In the midst of all the uncertainty about the future let us focus on the next thing the psalmist has to say: 'The Lord Almighty is with us; the God of Jacob is our fortress. Come and see the works of the Lord, the desolations he has brought on the earth.' Can you believe that? The psalmist equates God's works with desolation. Most of us would equate God's works with creation. But the psalmist sees a day coming when God will act in desolation. We talk about peace, but we are not peaceful people. It is the way of human nature that if we do not get our way by using our mouths, we will try to get it by the sword.

We think we are people of peace but just think over the last few years—about the Falklands War, or the Gulf War. One day, God will cause wars to cease. The psalmist puts it this way: 'He makes wars cease to the ends of the earth; he breaks the bow and shatters the spear, he burns the shields with fire.'

One day, when all the nations are ready with their high-tech weapons to go to war, God will make their combined wisdom and strength as nought. The psalmist says: 'come and see the works of the Lord...' It is as if the psalmist has been given a picture of final destruction. He is saying, 'Look: all the things that you trusted in—military, political, economic power—all are destroyed.' The climax is: 'Be still, and know that I am God...' Ultimately, God will be exalted in the whole earth.

The psalmist had things in perspective. He could say that God was his refuge and his strength. Regardless of appearances, regardless of his circumstances, the psalmist knew God was his refuge and his strength because he could see the world from God's perspective. He knew that his God was bigger than his circumstances. He knew his God was bigger than the problems around him. In a word, he knew God.

We need to have the same experience of God. In our

generation, I can go anywhere in Britain and say that Jesus is the way, the truth and the life and no one will mind. They may think I am narrow-minded but no one is likely to stone me; no one is going to kill me. Perhaps a day is coming when just to say that will be to sign your own death warrant.

Think about the history of Israel since the psalmist wrote this psalm. Israel has been dispersed among the nations. Only in 1948 did Israel—which had been apart for nearly 2,000 years—suddenly come together again. People came together from every nation to re-establish the land of Israel, in fulfilment of Old Testament prophecies. We need to watch and pray as we see what God is doing among the nations.

Prayer

Lord, thank you that you are the unchanging God, from everlasting to everlasting. In our world of change and uncertainty, thank you that we can depend on you. You are an ever-present help in times of trouble.

Thank you, Lord, that we can be confident for the future, with all its uncertainties, because we know that nothing can faze you. Amen

Psalm 73

A Psalm of Asaph.

Surely God is good to Israel,
  to those who are pure in heart.

But as for me, my feet had almost slipped;
  I had nearly lost my foothold.
For I envied the arrogant
  when I saw the prosperity of the wicked.

They have no struggles;
  their bodies are healthy and strong.
They are free from the burdens common to man;
  they are not plagued by human ills.
Therefore pride is their necklace;
  they clothe themselves with violence.
From their callous hearts comes iniquity;
  the evil conceits of their minds know no limits.
They scoff, and speak with malice;
  in their arrogance they threaten oppression.
Their mouths lay claim to heaven,
  and their tongues take possession of the earth.
Therefore their people turn to them
  and drink up waters in abundance.
They say, 'How can God know?
  Does the Most High have knowledge?'

This is what the wicked are like—
  always carefree, they increase in wealth.

Surely in vain have I kept my heart pure;
   in vain have I washed my hands in innocence.
All day long I have been plagued;
   I have been punished every morning.

If I had said, 'I will speak thus,'
   I would have betrayed your children.
When I tried to understand all this,
   it was oppressive to me
till I entered the sanctuary of God;
   then I understood their final destiny.

Surely you place them on slippery ground;
   you cast them down to ruin.
How suddenly are they destroyed,
   completely swept away by terrors!
As a dream when one awakes,
   so when you arise, O Lord,
   you will despise them as fantasies.

When my heart was grieved
   and my spirit embittered,
I was senseless and ignorant;
   I was a brute beast before you.

Yet I am always with you;
   you hold me by my right hand.
You guide me with your counsel,
   and afterwards you will take me into glory.
Whom have I in heaven but you?
   And earth has nothing I desire besides you.
My flesh and my heart may fail,
   but God is the strength of my heart
   and my portion forever.

Those who are far from you will perish;
   you destroy all who are unfaithful to you.
But as for me, it is good to be near God.
   I have made the Sovereign Lord my refuge;
   I will tell of all your deeds.

The psalm begins with a great opening salvo: 'Surely God is good to Israel, to those who are pure in heart.' When it says 'those who are pure in heart', it does not mean that they were good but rather that they had been called out by God, purified and set apart. In the same way, we have been called out by God. We are pure in heart in Christ, not in our own right.

This psalm is one of the wisdom psalms. It starts off with a proverb. What you need to understand is that a proverb speaks a truth which is from experience. This is the experience of Asaph, the writer. Asaph's starting-point is a belief that God is truly God to his people.

But all of a sudden there is a contradiction. Asaph was a community leader; he had been in David's court. Asaph was a top-dog psalmist but he is having problems in his thinking. He expresses his worries like this, 'But as for me, my feet had almost slipped; I had nearly lost my foothold. For I envied the arrogant when I saw the prosperity of the wicked.'

Asaph starts with a proverb, a statement which expresses a truth about God and then suddenly he juxtaposes it with his own experience, that is: 'I am good, but things aren't going well for me; they are bad, yet everything is going great for them.' Asaph is saying that the wicked are prospering and that is not the way things are supposed to go.

To understand this proverb we need to look at its *Sitz im Leben*—that is a fancy expression I learned in college.

It is German and means life-setting or context. To understand where Asaph is coming from, we need to look at Genesis chapter 12 verses 1–3.

> The Lord had said to Abram, 'Leave your country, your people and your father's household and go to the land I will show you.
>
> 'I will make you into a great nation
>   and I will bless you;
> I will make your name great,
>   and you will be a blessing.
> I will bless those who bless you,
>   and whoever curses you I will curse;
> and all peoples on earth
>   will be blessed through you.'

This passage is key to our understanding of the New Testament.

Asaph understood that God had given Abraham a mandate that would be fulfilled. Look at how God expresses himself. Six times he says, 'I will'. Abraham—or Abram, as he was still called at that time—was going to be blessed—not because he was a good guy and deserved it but because God said he would do it. Israel was to be blessed. Asaph understood this and believed God's promise. God was going to bless Israel.

To understand more of the background we need to look at Deuteronomy chapter 28 verses 1–2: 'If you fully obey the Lord your God and carefully follow all his commands I give you today, the Lord your God will set you high above all the nations on earth. All these blessings will come upon you and accompany you if you obey the Lord your God…'

There then follows a whole litany of blessings that God has for Israel and for those who obey him. The chapter also says in verses 15 onwards: 'However, if you do not obey the Lord your God and do not carefully follow all his commands and decrees I am giving you today, all these curses will come upon you and overtake you:'

Then there is a whole load of curses.

Asaph was a top-dog psalmist. He knew the background. He knew that God was good to those who were pure in heart. Yet he admitted that his feet had almost stumbled and his feet had almost slipped because his experience was at variance with what he believed. He admits: 'I envied the arrogant when I saw the prosperity of the wicked.'

We have had the proverb; we have had the lament. Now comes Asaph's sermon.

When I was in America, training as an athlete and following courses at Azusa University in California, I wrote a proverb: You can't know a picture unless you stand inside the frame. What I was trying to say was this: unless you have experienced something, you don't know what it's like. Many people may try to counsel you, but they have never been there. They don't know what they are talking about. You can't know the picture unless you are inside the frame.

My proverb expresses a truth from experience. However, it also contains a contradiction because it is also true that you cannot know a picture unless you stand outside the frame. Sometimes you are so involved that you cannot see the wood for the trees. You also need to stand outside the picture, to get the broader view, to be able to understand it.

Asaph knows the picture from the outside. He knows that God is good. Now he is in the middle of it and is learning from the inside whether God is good or not.

In verse 3 we see why his feet nearly slipped—because he was envious. As Asaph looks at the wicked, he sees their wealth. It seems that they do not have a care in the world. He looks at them and is envious.

In the 1980s it seemed to me that we were being encouraged by the government to be envious, and to look after number one—to improve ourselves and to grab as much as we could. Envy and greed can destroy us and pull us down.

The reason that Asaph's feet nearly slipped was that he took his eyes off God and what God was doing for him and put his eyes on what other people had. The grass often looks greener on the other side of the fence.

It is so easy to look at our neighbour's new car and to think, 'Look at that cool car. I wish I had a new car.' Your mind has forgotten the blessings of your own life and is hankering after what someone else has got.

Asaph had a lot going for him. He was loved. Yet in this moment, all he could see was what others had that he hadn't. Asaph could see the wicked rich doing things that he could not afford to do and he let it get to him.

Asaph goes on, 'They are free from the burdens common to man.' I am not sure that he was right in his assessment. Those people may look carefree on the outside, but you never know what is going on in their lives.

So Asaph protests: 'Surely in vain have I kept my heart pure; in vain have I washed my hands in innocence.' If people who do not obey God's Law prosper and are blessed, then I have wasted my time trying to be righteous and to live by God's standards.

Asaph couldn't get his head round it. He writes: 'When I tried to understand all this, it was oppressive to me.' It was worrying him and he couldn't see an answer.

He was in turmoil. Perhaps people were coming to him to ask him why God was not being faithful to his promises. Asaph had no answers for them.

If the psalm had finished here, Asaph's testimony would have been that God was not faithful. Thankfully, he didn't leave it there. The key to his understanding comes in verse 17: '…I entered the sanctuary of God; then I understood their final destiny.' This is the pivotal point of the psalm. Up to now Asaph has been thinking in terms of today and tomorrow, short-termism. He looks at these people, sees them with wads of banknotes and is envious.

At last, he comes into the sanctuary. It is not like us, perhaps coming to church, singing a few hymns, saying a few prayers—whether we mean them or not—and then going about our business for the rest of the week as if nothing had happened. Asaph comes crawling into the sanctuary, a man burdened. He is shouting to God, 'I don't understand it.' He is begging God for answers.

Then, all of a sudden, he sees the end. He has moved from the temporal to the eternal. God tells Asaph that it is about his perspective. From a short-term perspective there may seem to be a problem. When you see the big picture, everything falls into place.

Herodotus, the Greek historian in the 5th century BC, told a story about Croesus. One day Croesus was standing there feeling pleased with himself, thinking, 'Can there ever have been a happier guy than I?' Then a famous Greek philosopher named Solon arrived from Athens.

Croesus asked Solon, 'Can there be anyone happier than me?' Solon replied that the happiest person he knew was one who was prosperous, had children, lived to see his children's children and then died in battle and was given a monumental funeral by his friends. Croesus said, 'OK, maybe him, but apart from him can anyone else possibly be happier than me?' Solon replied, 'There were twin boys who were athletic but who died at a young age because when their mother needed to get somewhere and her chariot broke down, the boys pulled her along and got her there on time. They died in the prime of life and everyone said how wonderful they were.'

Croesus was perplexed. How could Solon put these people ahead of him? Solon replied, 'At the moment, your prosperity doesn't impress me. Many things can happen between now and the end of your life. I would need to see the end of your life before I could place you with the others.'

Asaph, our psalmist, realized in that moment in the temple that the rich may be wealthy now, but, 'What good is it for a man to gain the whole world, yet forfeit his soul?' (Mark 8:36) For the Christian, too, true happiness can only come at the end of life, when we stand before our Maker and hear him say, 'Well done, good and faithful servant.'

Is Asaph's conclusion wishful thinking? No—it's prophetic. No matter how rich you are on earth, when you come face to face with the living Lord, you have nothing. It is as if Asaph is saying that life is just a dream; reality is still to come. The apostle Paul put it like this: 'Now we see but a poor reflection as in a mirror; then we shall see face to face. Now I know in part; then I shall know fully, even as I am fully known.' (1 Corinthians 13:12)

Asaph realized that his perspective was all wrong. He says: 'I was senseless and ignorant; I was a brute beast before you.'

As you may know, I have a dog—a Doberman called Dillinger—and he is crazy. We go out for walks. He likes to chase rabbits, hares, even deer. He never catches anything! Sometimes I can see a hare quite close by while my dog is rushing around, smelling where the hare was half an hour ago. He's off the pace.

That is what Asaph is saying. He was like a wild, ignorant dog, racing around yet missing the point. The point was in eternity and he was rushing around in temporality. Asaph was foolish, like an animal.

Asaph feels stupid and unworthy, but even in his crisis he realizes that God is faithful: 'Yet I am always with you; you hold me by my right hand. You guide me with your counsel, and afterwards you will take me into glory.'

I don't need to chase more and more material things. If I have got my relationship with God sorted out, the rest can take care of itself. Even in death Asaph realizes that in God he will live forever. He had a new perspective, an eternal perspective.

You may be going through a hard time at the moment. You need to live each day as it comes. You need to be thankful for what you have got. Where Asaph went wrong in the first place was that he looked at other people, rather than being content with his own position. He looked at other people when he should have looked at God.

Prayer

*Heavenly Father, thank you for your Word. Help us when
we go through hard times, when life does not make sense,
when we feel burdened. Be with us and strengthen us.
Be with us as you were with Asaph. Make sense in a
senseless life. Give us that perspective of eternity. Help us
to live each day as it comes. Help us to see the blessings
you have poured into our lives. Help us not to be envious
of others but to be grateful for what you have given us.
Help us, even when things are hard, to give glory to you
in the way we live our lives. May we be Christlike
reflectors of you. We ask this in your matchless and holy
name. Amen*

Psalm 85

For the director of music. Of the Sons of Korah.
A psalm.

You showed favour to your land, O Lord;
* you restored the fortunes of Jacob.*
You forgave the iniquity of your people
* and covered all their sins. Selah*

You set aside all your wrath
* and turned from your fierce anger.*

Restore us again, O God our Saviour,
* and put away your displeasure towards us.*
Will you be angry with us for ever?
* Will you prolong your anger through all generations?*
Will you not revive us again,
* that your people may rejoice in you?*
Show us your unfailing love, O Lord,
* and grant us your salvation.*

I will listen to what God the Lord will say;
* he promises peace to his people, his saints—*
*   but let them not return to folly.*
Surely his salvation is near those who fear him,
* that his glory may dwell in our land.*

Love and faithfulness meet together;
* righteousness and peace kiss each other.*
Faithfulness springs forth from the earth,
* and righteousness looks down from heaven.*

The Lord will indeed give what is good,
   and our land will yield its harvest.
Righteousness goes before him
   and prepares the way for his steps.

This is a wonderful psalm. It can be categorized as a descriptive psalm. In verse 1 notice the words:

'*You* showed favour to *your* land, O Lord; *you* restored the fortunes of Jacob. *You* forgave the iniquity of *your* people and covered all their sins. *You* set aside all *your* wrath and turned from *your* fierce anger.'

You, you, you, you. The psalmist was describing what God had done for Israel in the past. The psalmist was an individual but he was well aware of the corporate history of Israel. He was aware of the past. He understood the importance of the exodus. He knew about God's dealing with Jacob. He knew the favour of God which had been shown to the people and to the land.

I wonder if we are as familiar with our history? Do we know our church history? Do we know about Constantine? Do we understand the significance of the Reformation? What about secular history—the Renaissance, the Industrial Revolution, the rise of capitalism? Do we know how all these events affect us today?

The psalmist understood his nation's history and what God had done and how God had restored them and led them through the centuries. He understood how Israel had got to where she was.

He acknowledged that Israel had sinned, but he was also aware of God's forgiveness. He could look back and see how Israel had sinned and had fallen but how God had forgiven and restored his people. The psalmist knew what had happened in the past, so it gave him faith that God could do it again. Do we have that sort of faith? If we studied church history, we would be able to see how many times the church had failed and fallen and yet God had restored it.

Do we think about how God has kept and restored the Church over the last thousand years? Do we believe he can do the same for us?

Note how the psalmist identified with what has gone before. He didn't say, 'They did this.' He said, 'We did this.' It is very difficult for modern men and women to get beyond thinking of 'I, me, myself' and to think what the past has got to do with them.

The psalmist recognized that the people had sinned, that they had fallen, but that God had acted and restored them to their land. What had God done? He had restored their fortunes and brought them back into the land. He had forgiven their iniquity. But he had not just forgiven it; he had covered it. I love that idea about covering. There is a heap of stinking, smouldering garbage there and God has covered it.

What did God cover it with? With the blood of Christ. It is covered, dealt with. It cannot be seen any more. You just see Christ standing there, having dealt with it.

The psalmist understood how many times God had covered their sin. He had 'set aside all… [his] wrath and turned from… [his] fierce anger.'

Do we have that sense of corporate identity, of continuity with the Church throughout history? Do we appreciate our heritage? Do we know where we are coming from? Do we understand what effect our society has on us? The psalmist certainly did. He asked God to restore the nation again.

The word 'restore' reminds me of my first car—my Opel LTJ, my cool, swift, debonair, happening, red sports car. When I bought that car I did not even have a driving licence. But I had faith. I knew that one day I would drive.

I had saved up my money and when I was sixteen-and-a-half, in the army in Germany, I bought this car. For six months it just sat there and I paid people to restore it. It had shining, steel-rimmed wheels. It had a leather steering-wheel, pop-up lights. It was wicked wheels! It was better than brand new because I had restored it.

That is what the psalmist is saying: 'Restore us... make us better than we were before. Restore us to more than our former glory. Make us stand out.'

After the Babylonian exile, when Cyrus, King of Persia, captured Babylon and allowed people to leave, some Jews started coming back to Israel. But a lot of them had big wealth and did not want to go.

Those who returned were just sitting there, bemoaning the fact that it wasn't as pretty as it used to be— 'There used to be a temple here.' Some of the people, however, said, 'Let's do something. Let us restore it.'

'Restore us again, O God our Saviour, and put away your displeasure toward us. Will you be angry with us for ever? Will you prolong your anger through all generations? Will you not revive us again, that your people may rejoice in you? Show us your unfailing love, O Lord, and grant us your salvation.'

God's 'unfailing love' is an important concept. The Hebrew word is *hesed*—faithfulness, loving-kindness, a contract from God. God makes an agreement that he is going to love you and go on loving you. Why? Because he loves you! He never stops loving you.

When it's all gone wrong and you are stinking, hiding in a corner, thinking that you are useless, God still loves you. He loves you and he loves you and he loves you. I know that is very hard for us to fathom. We do not experience that kind of love anywhere else. His Word is filled with examples of that love.

The psalmist was fortunate because he understood it. When he asked God: 'Will you be angry with us for ever?' he knew the answer. He was thinking, 'It is impossible, God, for you to remain angry. I know that because I know my history and I know how you acted in the past.'

One good example is Solomon, who asked God for wisdom and God gave him great wisdom. Solomon later went and chased after women and finished up with thousands of wives and as many gods. Yet God still blessed him and brought him back again, when he repented. (See, for example, 1 Kings 11; 2 Chronicles 7.)

The psalmist knew his stories. He understood the situation in his own life. He implores you and me to look at our own life and to see that when we fall, God is still there. We can turn back. In my own life, the times when I feel closest to God are the times when I have fallen and have then come back to God and been forgiven and restored.

In those times when you realize how far you have strayed from God, how you have compromised your first love but God has restored you to your former glory and beyond, then, hopefully, too, you have learned from the experience. You have learned more and have been restored more. That is the idea here.

The writer is certain that God is going to restore his people. He knows that God is always there, that it is the people who have moved away from God, not the other way round. Revive us, Lord!

'Will you prolong your anger through all generations? Will you not revive us again, that your people may rejoice in you?'

I was struck by the reference to 'all generations', which speaks to us about corporate unity and continuity. On the one hand, the writer understands his history and knows what has gone on in the past, but he is also aware of the present and the future when he talks about 'all generations'. He is aware that what is happening now will affect posterity. Have we the same awareness of what we are passing on to other generations?

The psalmist is saying, 'If God does not restore us, if all I see around me is despondency, what kind of message about God do I have to pass on to future generations?' He wants God to do something in his generation that can be passed on to future generations.

We need to be able to talk about our experience of God today, a vibrant, living experience. We cannot just rely on past experiences when God did something for us. Our experience must be up to date—this week I was lost, but God found me.

The psalmist says, 'I will listen to what God the Lord will say'. Listening to God is so important. I am sure that it was no accident that God gave us two ears but only one mouth. If only we could learn to use them in the right proportions, we would go a long way.

Up to now, the emphasis has been on the corporate, the unity. Now it becomes personal, 'I will'. The writer will listen to God because he knows what God has promised; '...he promises peace to his people, his saints—but let them not return to folly.'

When I first became a Christian, my prayers were very much a monologue. In the morning I would pray, 'Heavenly Father, I love you so much. Thank you for my salvation. Bless him and him, bless this, bless that. Blah, blah, blah. See ya!' and off I went to work. At the end of the day, I would thank God for a good day and then fall asleep. What was missing from my prayers was that I never stopped to listen.

What I need to do more is to come to God in humility and say, 'Here am I, teach me. Tell me what I need to know.' And then just sit and listen. I have learned over the years that if I sit quietly and listen, God can do so much more.

People ask me, how I know that God is speaking to me? Well, this is how I know. He promises peace to his people. Often when I put something to God, if I am struggling with the issues, then I know that is not what he wants me to do. It is when he lays his peace—that passes all understanding—in my heart, that I know it is God's will. He may bring someone to me who says something, confirms something and he gives me peace. I pick up the Word and read something and—BOOM!— he gives me peace.

Peace is a great indicator of God's presence in your life. Listen to God and you will have peace in your life.

'Surely his salvation is near those who fear him...' In Proverbs we read: 'The fear of the Lord is the beginning of wisdom.' (Proverbs 9:10) We are to 'work out... [our] salvation with fear and trembling' (Philippians 2:12) but the starting-point is to fear God.

We are told to listen to God to hear his Word, 'that his glory may dwell in our land'. If you know God and you have peace and you can tell people what he is doing in your life, that is great. But there is no point in telling other people about God if you have no peace in your own life, no experience of God in your own life. There will be trouble to face, but God has said that we can go to him with our problems and he will give us peace.

'Love and faithfulness meet together; righteousness and peace kiss each other.' What does the psalmist's picture here say to us? Do you know the peace of God? His righteousness comes down and covers all your sins. His love comes down and conquers all. Are you faithful to the Lord? Do you feel his heart beating? Do you see him as he draws you to his side with the blood splashing down his hands, as he covers all your sins? So that when you stand before God you don't stand there in your sins but covered by his righteousness?

I am touched by this verse because kissing is such an intimate thing. If I can use an illustration from my own life, when my wife is pleased with me, she kisses me. But that is not the sweetest kiss I get from her.

Sometimes I am in her bad books, when I have been out at work all day and rush in: 'Hiya Monika! Hello kids!' but before they have time to answer, I am out again with my sports bag to play tennis or something. Then I get back late and next morning, dash off to work again—just thinking about myself. But when I finally manage to pluck up the courage to admit that I was wrong and she forgives me, the kiss that follows is the sweetest kiss. It is almost worth the grief, just to get that kiss! That kiss communicates that she has forgiven me.

That is what the psalmist wants, what he has been promised. God promises to get close in the grime of your life, not where the glitz and glamour is, but where the grit and grime is. God is a forgiving God.

'Faithfulness springs forth from the earth.' Faithfulness may make us think about works, about you trying to please God, doing everything that you think God would want you to do. So often we think about works as earning our salvation, which, of course, we cannot do.

But look at the context: faithfulness is not you trying to get God's love; it is a response to God's love. It is you acknowledging that God loves you. Because he loves you, you want to please him. Why is it that 'Faithfulness springs forth from the earth?'—Because 'righteousness looks down from heaven', because of what Jesus has done as he covers your sin and brings you back to God.

God has poured out his righteousness but he asks you to be faithful. He asks you to acknowledge your sin, to get up and turn from your sin and ask his forgiveness. Go to him as to a loving father and say, 'I have sinned.' His response will be to say, 'I have covered your sin. Get up.'

Peter is such a good example of this. I love Peter because he was rash, spontaneous, emotional, hard-headed, and I identify with that. What do we learn from Peter about love and faithfulness and peace?

Remember the time that Jesus washed the disciples' feet. When he came to Peter, Peter said, 'No… you shall never wash my feet.' Jesus answered, 'Unless I wash you, you have no part with me.' 'Then, Lord,' Simon Peter replied, 'not just my feet but my hands and my head as well!' (John 13:8–9)

Jesus was taking care of the disciples but he was also setting them an example. He continued: 'You call me "Teacher" and "Lord," and rightly so, for that is what I am. Now that I, your Lord and Teacher, have washed your feet, you also should wash one another's feet. I have set you an example that you should do as I have done for you.' (John 13:13–15)

Later that evening Jesus was to tell the disciples that one of them would betray him. Peter was to deny that he even knew Jesus. When Peter realized what he had done he broke down and cried. Did he realize that just hours ago, his Lord had washed his feet and cleansed him? He had promised not to let Jesus down. When Jesus was crucified, Peter was still carrying his guilt that in the crisis he had let Jesus down.

A week later, Jesus, risen from the dead, has this encounter with Peter: 'When they had finished eating, Jesus said to Simon Peter, "Simon son of John, do you truly love me more than these?"

'"Yes, Lord," he said, "you know that I love you."

'Jesus said, "Feed my lambs."

'Again Jesus said, "Simon son of John, do you truly love me?"

'He answered, "Yes, Lord, you know that I love you."

'Jesus said, "Take care of my sheep."

'The third time he said to him, "Simon son of John, do you love me?"

'Peter was hurt because Jesus asked him the third time, "Do you love me?" He said, "Lord, you know all things; you know that I love you."

'Jesus said, "Feed my sheep. I tell you the truth, when you were younger you dressed yourself and went where you wanted; but when you are old you will stretch out your hands, and someone else will dress you and lead you where you do not want to go." Jesus said this to indicate the kind of death by which Peter would glorify God. Then he said to him, "Follow me!"' (John 21:15–19)

Peter has to realize that Jesus' love requires his faithfulness. In that realization, Peter receives God's peace.

I would suggest that many people reading this book will recognize that scenario, when we have been like Peter, when we have had our Peter-moments. Jesus wants you to feed his lambs.

You know there are times when you are his sheep and he will feed you and there will also be times when you will be feeding others. Jesus loves you. He has given you his righteousness. Be faithful to him. Have his peace.

Prayer

Father, we thank you that you are God who restores us. Like the psalmist, like Peter, we fall into sin. We need you to forgive and restore us. Thank you, Father, that you have promised not to be angry for ever. Help us to turn from our sins, to accept your forgiveness and restoration and to go forward with you. Help us, Father, as you forgive us and feed us, to serve and feed others in your church. In Jesus' name. Amen

Psalm 109

For the director of music. Of David. A psalm.

O God, whom I praise,
  do not remain silent,
for wicked and deceitful men
  have opened their mouths against me;
  they have spoken against me with lying tongues.
With words of hatred they surround me;
  they attack me without cause.
In return for my friendship they accuse me,
  but I am a man of prayer.
They repay me evil for good,
  and hatred for my friendship.

Appoint an evil man to oppose him;
  let an accuser stand at his right hand.
When he is tried, let him be found guilty,
  and may his prayers condemn him.
May his days be few;
  may another take his place of leadership.
May his children be fatherless
  and his wife a widow.
May his children be wandering beggars;
  may they be driven from their ruined homes.
May a creditor seize all he has;
  may strangers plunder the fruits of his labour.
May no one extend kindness to him
  or take pity on his fatherless children.
May his descendants be cut off,
  their names blotted out from the next generation.

May the iniquity of his fathers be
　　remembered before the Lord;
　　may the sin of his mother never be blotted out.
May their sins always remain before the Lord,
　　that he may cut off the memory of them from the earth.

For he never thought of doing a kindness,
　　but hounded to death the poor
　　and the needy and the broken-hearted.
He loved to pronounce a curse—
　　may it come on him;
he found no pleasure in blessing—may it be far from him.
He wore cursing as his garment;
　　it entered into his body like water,
　　into his bones like oil.
May it be like a cloak wrapped about him,
　　like a belt tied for ever round him.
May this be the Lord's payment to my accusers,
　　to those who speak evil of me.

But you, O Sovereign Lord,
　　deal well with me for your name's sake;
　　out of the goodness of your love, deliver me.
For I am poor and needy,
　　and my heart is wounded within me.
I fade away like an evening shadow;
　　I am shaken off like a locust.
My knees give way from fasting;
　　my body is thin and gaunt.
I am an object of scorn to my accusers;
　　when they see me, they shake their heads.

Help me, O Lord my God;
　　save me in accordance with your love.

Let them know that it is your hand,
  that you, O Lord, have done it.
They may curse, but you will bless;
  when they attack they will be put to shame,
  but your servant will rejoice.
My accusers will be clothed with disgrace
  and wrapped in shame as in a cloak.

With my mouth I will greatly extol the Lord;
  in the great throng I will praise him.
For he stands at the right hand of the needy one,
  to save his life from those who condemn him.

One reason why I love the Psalms is because they contain real theology. It is not theology derived from first principles. It is not someone sitting in an ivory tower saying, 'If God is this, therefore that.' It is, rather, the theology of someone who has a relationship with God expressing the vibrancy of that relationship.

If something hurts, they express the hurt to God; if something makes them happy, they express the happiness of that moment to God. In the Psalms we find the very heartbeat of the individual. The Psalms give us a real picture of the life of the psalmist. In the Psalms we meet the real God of the real person.

The psalmist introduces himself as a man of prayer who praises God in the midst of a tough situation. My reading of the word 'Praise' is that David is saying to God, 'I have talked to you on many occasions. I have seen you work in my life, so I have been able to stand up and give a praise report in the congregation.'

The psalm starts: 'O God, whom I praise, do not remain silent.' David tells us that he is a man of prayer and praise, but at this moment in time this God who is vibrant, who is alive and kicking, who works in his life, this God would appear to be dead. It was a period in David's life when God appeared to be silent.

Ironically, at the time when God is silent, everyone else is speaking to him—and he does not like what he hears. It is an unfortunate juxtaposition. The God he loves and serves is silent but the people whose opinions he does not really care for have a lot to say!

David is saying: 'They can say what they like about me, but I am a man of prayer.' We have to acknowledge that this is a one-sided argument. We only see it from David's point of view. If we could ask the other people, they might give us a completely different account of the dispute. David has a complaint against someone but, for all we know, that person might have an equally big complaint against David.

In the psalm David elaborates his complaints against this person, who has no opportunity or right of reply. As I have made clear earlier, I do not like David but I do admire him greatly.

I can't help asking the question, 'What does David mean by friendship?' Was Uriah a friend of David? Remember Uriah?—a companion of David when he was in the wilderness—but when David wanted Uriah's wife, Bathsheba, he did not let the friendship stand in his way. He even went as far as to have Uriah killed (2 Samuel 11). If that is David's idea of friendship, then I wouldn't want to be his friend!

There was a king of Gath called Achish. David made friends with him when he needed him. Then later, he caused trouble for Achish along his borders. David was double-dealing and double-crossing Achish (1 Samuel 27). If that kind of double-dealing is David's idea of friendship, he can keep it!

There are other examples that we could look at—his wife Michal, Joab and so on. But I have seen enough to convince me that I do not like David's idea of friendship. Neither, it would appear, did the fellow in this psalm.

David is clearly upset at the actions of this so-called friend, so he asks for him to be dealt with. He does not mince his words against this man: 'Appoint an evil man to oppose him; let an accuser stand at his right hand. When he is tried, let him be found guilty, and may his prayers condemn him. May his days be few; may another take his place of leadership. May his children be fatherless and his wife a widow. May his children be wandering beggars; may they be driven from their ruined homes.'

David is confident that God will answer his prayers. However, the other man is praying too. When I was competing in athletics, people used to asked me if I prayed about races and what would happen if there was another Christian in the race; would God have a problem over whose prayer to answer!

David is saying, 'God, you have a problem! He says he knows you. I say I know him and I ask that his prayers will condemn him. So what are you going to do?' David knows that in the past God has answered his prayers and he is confident that on this occasion God will again answer his prayer.

Even though God has been silent lately, he remains confident that God will answer his prayers and in answering David's prayers, will condemn the other guy by not answering his prayers. In essence he is saying, 'Answer my prayers! Don't answer his prayers!'

As David continues, it is heavy stuff. David is almost calling down curses on this guy and all his household and family. David prays fourteen requests introduced by 'may'. David is asking for this guy to be blotted out of his life permanently, almost that it will be as if he had never existed.

David's faith is admirable. He is making a big request and he is doing it publicly. If this does not happen, David will look a bit silly—to put it mildly. But he has confidence that God will answer his prayer.

In verse 17 David says: 'He loved to pronounce a curse—may it come on him…' Now isn't that a bit rich! For the past eleven verses what has David been doing, if it is not invoking a curse on this man? And now what does he accuse him of, but of loving to pronounce curses! Was he speaking with forked tongue?

David continues with his tirade against this man: 'He wore cursing as his garment; it entered into his body like water, into his bones like oil. May it be like a cloak wrapped about him, like a belt tied for ever round him.'

David is obsessed with him. He cannot stop thinking about him. The more he goes on, the more David begins to sound like the one he is criticizing. It is interesting that we become like the things we hate. David is being dragged down to the level of his adversary.

David then turns to plead with God: 'But you, O Sovereign Lord, deal well with me for your name's sake; out of the goodness of your love, deliver me… Help me, O Lord my God; save me in accordance with your love.'

David describes himself as 'poor and needy'. That reminds us of 1 Samuel chapter 18 verse 23, where David says, 'I'm only a poor man and little known,' when David is a young man in the household of Saul. Saul is elsewhere referred to as David's enemy. Could this be the context of the psalm? Could Saul be the enemy David is referring to in this psalm? We cannot be sure, but it certainly fits.

David was the eighth son in the family. He should have known his place. Perhaps he was a bit conceited.

We are told in the Bible that David was a man after God's own heart (Acts 13:22). Think about that. Even though he was very self-centred, a murderer and an adulterer, we are told that he was a man after God's own heart.

Even though he cheated and double-crossed, he loved God and always returned to God. He was a fearless leader, but when he became a king he realized how much more there was to it. When he found himself in charge, he found it was more difficult than he thought it would be.

I think it is the same in church life. It is much easier to see what is wrong with our church than to have the courage to lead the church through the problem and put it right.

When I realized that because I was a child of God I was accepted and did not need to prove anything to anyone, it freed me. It was liberating. I am sure that David found his security in his relationship with God in his difficulties. In the midst of his darkness, he was able to hold on to the reality that God was with him.

Life is full of ups and downs, but if we realize that God is in control, we will have a security to carry us through. What I admire about David is that he believed in God; he talked to God; he walked with God and God was his. God was not a vague concept. God was a present reality who walked with him every day.

Prayer

*Heavenly Father, we thank you for the example of David.
Thank you that the Bible shows us David, warts and all.
Thank you for the encouragement we can find in the life
of David, that in the middle of his troubles he still clung
on to you. In all things that he did, he came back to you.
Father, we pray that, like David, we too may have a living
and vibrant God and that we too may hear from you and
trust in you and know that you will come to our aid.
Amen*

Psalm 145

A psalm of praise. Of David.

I will exalt you, my God the King;
  I will praise your name for ever and ever.
Every day I will praise you
  and extol your name for ever and ever.

Great is the Lord and most worthy of praise;
  his greatness no one can fathom.
One generation will commend your works to another;
  they will tell of your mighty acts.
They will speak of the glorious splendour of your majesty,
  and I will meditate on your wonderful works.
They will tell of the power of your awesome works,
  and I will proclaim your great deeds.
They will celebrate your abundant goodness
  and joyfully sing of your righteousness.

The Lord is gracious and compassionate,
  slow to anger and rich in love.
The Lord is good to all;
  he has compassion on all he has made.
All you have made will praise you, O Lord;
  your saints will extol you.
They will tell of the glory of your kingdom
  and speak of your might,
so that all men may know of your mighty acts
  and the glorious splendour of your kingdom.
Your kingdom is an everlasting kingdom,
  and your dominion endures through all generations.

The Lord is faithful to all his promises
and loving towards all he has made.
The Lord upholds all those who fall
and lifts up all who are bowed down.
The eyes of all look to you,
and you give them their food at the proper time.
You open your hand
and satisfy the desires of every living thing.

The Lord is righteous in all his ways
and loving towards all he has made.
The Lord is near to all who call on him,
to all who call on him in truth.
He fulfils the desires of those who fear him;
he hears their cry and saves them.
The Lord watches over all who love him,
but all the wicked he will destroy.

My mouth will speak in praise of the Lord.
Let every creature praise his holy name
for ever and ever.

Before we get stuck into this psalm, let me remind you
of the context. When Samuel was about to die, he had a
final meeting with the leaders of the people. It went like
this:

So all the elders of Israel gathered together and came to
Samuel at Ramah. They said to him, 'You are old, and
your sons do not walk in your ways; now appoint a king
to lead us, such as all the other nations have.'
But when they said, 'Give us a king to lead us,' this
displeased Samuel; so he prayed to the Lord. And the
Lord told him: 'Listen to all that the people are saying to

*you; it is not you they have rejected, but they have rejected
me as their king. As they have done from the day I
brought them up out of Egypt until this day, forsaking me
and serving other gods, so they are doing to you. Now
listen to them; but warn them solemnly and let them
know what the king who will reign over them will do.'*

*Samuel told all the words of the Lord to the people
who were asking him for a king. He said, 'This is what
the king who will reign over you will do: He will take your
sons and make them serve with his chariots and horses,
and they will run in front of his chariots. Some he will
assign to be commanders of thousands and commanders
of fifties, and others to plough his ground and reap his
harvest, and still others to make weapons of war and
equipment for his chariots. He will take your daughters to
be perfumers and cooks and bakers. He will take the best
of your fields and vineyards and olive groves and give
them to his attendants. He will take a tenth of your
grain and of your vintage and give it to his officials and
attendants. Your menservants and maidservants and the
best of your cattle and donkeys he will take for his own
use. He will take a tenth of your flocks, and you yourselves
will become his slaves. When that day comes, you will cry
out for relief from the king you have chosen, and the Lord
will not answer you in that day.'*

*But the people refused to listen to Samuel. 'No!' they
said. 'We want a king over us. Then we shall be like all
the other nations, with a king to lead us and to go out
before us and fight our battles.'* (1 Samuel 8:4–20)

The passages in Samuel remind us of how it came about
that Israel had a king. Samuel tries to warn them that
what they think is freedom may, in fact, turn out to be
bondage, if they want to serve earthly kings.

The Israelites looked around them and saw that other nations had kings who led them into battle. They saw kings providing for their people but what they did not see was the cost of serving those kings.

Maybe God intended to give them a king but it would be in his time. They wanted a king now. They wanted a king like the nations around them. Samuel, following God's instructions, gives them the king they want. As we know, in due course, the kingdom was ripped from Saul—but the damage had been done.

From that moment on, factions broke out. The people who until now had known only God as their king, broke into factions. I believe that it is the same in our lives. God is indeed our King but he gives us the choice to serve earthly kings if we prefer. But those earthly kings, rather than giving us freedom, will bring us bondage. Like the people around us, we will be enslaved to the things of this world.

In Psalm 145 we meet David, of whom the scriptures say, 'He was a man after God's own heart.' Now, as I've said before, when I read about David in Samuel and Kings, I do not like the man I see. He comes across as a manipulator, a usurper, a man who is very crafty, who always gets his own way. David is just not a nice guy. He steals people's wives. He has a raving party and extorts money and food. I don't like David.

But when I read the Psalms I begin to understand why the scriptures say he was a man after God's own heart (Acts 13:22). I think it means that not only did he have the heartbeat of God but that he also strove after God.

Even though he had flaws in his character, he only served one king, God Almighty. In his weakness, he went to God for his strength. The things I don't like in David are things that I see in myself. In David I see my flaws and my weaknesses—for example, the times I want to usurp people's authority.

'I will exalt you, my God the King; I will praise your name for ever and ever. Every day I will praise you and extol your name for ever and ever.'

Note the opening words, 'I will'. In fact, five times in the psalm, he uses this phrase. David was the king—and Israel knew no greater king than David—but notice how he addresses God as king. He willingly subordinates himself to God, his king. Remember that the people had chanted, 'Saul has slain his thousands and David his tens of thousands.' (1 Samuel 18:7) This was a huge statement for David. He was a living icon.

Everybody wanted to be like David. But David knew deep down that he was not how he wanted to be. David would serve no earthly king but looked rather towards God to be his king.

The words 'Every day I will praise you' are a challenge to me. I remember when I first became a Christian, every morning I got up and the first move was to read the Bible. As time has gone on, my time with God has tended to be marginalized to any time in the day when I could grab a quick five minutes. I am challenged to an act of will to apportion time in my day to God.

Isn't there a challenge in this psalm for all of us to start the day with an acknowledgment of 'my God the King'? David promised to affirm God as his king every day.

'Great is the Lord and most worthy of praise; his greatness no one can fathom.' Someone recently said something very profound in my hearing. It was this: modern man is great with technology but small with wisdom. I think that is so true. Think about the technical achievements of the modern world—mobile phones that work almost anywhere in the world, laptop computers which interface with other computers around the world. We are technological giants but spiritual pygmies. God's greatness is infinite. By comparison, our achievements are very limited.

'One generation will commend your works to another; they will tell of your mighty acts.' This verse has become very meaningful to me recently. My daughter has been asking a lot of questions about God and I have come to see that she is going to get most of the answers, in the first instance, from me—'one generation will commend your works to another.' One generation is a spiritual life-giver to another. I am entrusted with passing God's truth on to the next generation.

Look at the Bible, in which we have thousands of years of wisdom passed down to us from generation to generation. The Bible is low in technology but high in wisdom. We, in turn, are charged with the task of passing the message on to the next generation.

Note, too, David's use of the word 'meditate'. We are not to rush off and hurriedly regurgitate what someone else has said to us. We are to meditate on it, think it through, made it our own and then pass it on. We are to take the time to work the message out in our own lives before we pass it on.

As we meditate on what has been passed on to us, just think of the millions still to come, who will also celebrate the greatness of God. It would be good for us to stop and thank God for those in the past who have helped us along the way to faith.

David was aware of his heritage. He was aware of his responsibility to the people he ruled over. He wanted to make sure they also served God.

I once heard a story of a brilliant pastor, a clever man,

a great preacher. His church grew from a mere dozen to a congregation of hundreds. He was in great demand as a speaker at other churches.

One day a man came to a church service. You could smell this man way before you saw him. His foul breath was surpassed only by his bad language. He emitted noise from every orifice. Dandruff the size of snowflakes fell constantly from his head. I think you get the picture—he was bad news.

Every Sunday he took the same seat and each week there were fewer people in the vicinity. A year went by and the numbers attending the church shrank from eight hundred at the height to just over one hundred. Why did the pastor not act? Why did he allow the man to belch and burp and moan and groan? The only positive thing the man ever said was, 'Thank you, Jesus.' and in fact he said that so often that it became a curse more than a blessing.

One week, the situation was different. The hundred empty chairs had something missing from their epicentre—no stink, no belch, no 'Thank you, Jesus.' Afterwards, the congregation congratulated the pastor on another barnstorming performance, but his mind was not on the platitudes of the day. His day had not been complete without 'Thank you, Jesus'.

On his way home, he took a detour to the derelict house where the man lived. It was easy to find; he just followed his nose. On arrival, the door was ajar. On entering, he worked his way through the rooms, calling out, 'Hello! Anyone there?' Eventually, he heard a faint, 'Thank you, Jesus.'

The man had suffered a stroke. With no friends, no relatives, he lay there waiting to die. The pastor heaved the stinking body into a comfortable position and attended to the man's every need. Of course, being in America, no doctor came, as the man was not insured. Every day for a year, the pastor fed him, bathed him and left him with a prayer.

Quite when it was that the deed changed from labour to love the pastor did not know, but when the man died in his arms, the pastor said, 'Thank you, Jesus.' In the end, the pastor had been enriched by the man's appearance at church because he had learned about God's grace in a practical way.

That man showed in one hour all the breadth and depth of our depravity when he came into the church service, but the pastor showed the depth of Christ's love. For if anyone knew us like Jesus knows us they would see that our thoughts, words and deeds are continually evil. Jesus knows our innermost parts and that man who came into the sanctuary was really very much like us. We are very respectable on the outside but deep down Jesus sees the inner person and feeds us, loves us, prays over us.

David reminds me of the man in that story. There was a bad smell when he was around. Some of the things he did brought no credit on him, but God cared for him, loved him, restored him. That is why we see God's compassion revealed in the Psalms. David was fully aware that he stank and he belched and he groaned and all those things but, each and every time he was not ashamed to wear sackcloth and ashes and to repent, to shave his head in front of the congregation and to say, in modern day vernacular, 'Thank you, Jesus.'

In the next few verses we get a picture of the God that David was going to pass on to the generations. It is not a God who is waiting to slap you and beat you when you get anything wrong, but a God who is ready to forgive.

Seven times, David illuminates the character of God

in describing him to future generations. Look at how his words describe God: 'abundant goodness... righteousness... gracious... compassionate... slow to anger and rich in love'. God always thinks the best of you. He is always wanting to give. This is the God David is passing on to future generations. This is the God I need to tell my daughter about. God is not like me. He doesn't get upset; he doesn't get ratty; he doesn't nitpick. He is gracious and loving. He is gracious even to those who do not know him.

God does not 'do' graciousness. He does not 'do' goodness. He *is* goodness. He *is* graciousness. If God had not become man, people could have said that he did not really understand, but Jesus became man and lived among us, stank with us, lived with lepers and drunkards.

God is faithful. He has entered into a covenant with us and he will keep it. He is constant and dependable. 'The Lord is righteous...' That means he is just, blameless, pure. None of us are righteous of ourselves, but the Bible says that God imputes his righteousness to us. 'The Lord is near...' He is near, accessible and available to all who call on him.

'The Lord watches over all who love him...' I have already mentioned my dog. When he is with me, he watches my every move. Nothing gets past my dog. In a similar way, nothing gets past God's eyes.

Are you beginning to see the God David knew? Can you see now why David was called a man after God's own heart? Can you see how the bad times in his life helped him get near to God?

'My mouth will speak in praise of the Lord. Let every creature praise his holy name for ever and ever.' There is a challenge for all of us.

Prayer

Heavenly Father, thank you that you are good, righteous, gracious and compassionate. Thank you, Lord, that you are slow to anger and rich in love. You are most worthy of all our praise. Help us, Lord, along with the psalmist, to praise your holy name for ever. Amen

Deuteronomy 32:1–43

The Song of Moses

Listen, O heavens, and I will speak;
hear, O earth, the words of my mouth.
Let my teaching fall like rain
and my words descend like dew,
like showers on new grass,
like abundant rain on tender plants.

I will proclaim the name of the Lord.
Oh, praise the greatness of our God!
He is the Rock, his works are perfect,
and all his ways are just.
A faithful God who does no wrong,
upright and just is he.

They have acted corruptly towards him;
to their shame they are no longer his children,
but a warped and crooked generation.
Is this the way you repay the Lord,
O foolish and unwise people?
Is he not your Father, your Creator,
who made you and formed you?

Remember the days of old;
consider the generations long past.
Ask your father and he will tell you,
your elders, and they will explain to you.

When the Most High gave the nations their inheritance,
    when he divided all mankind,
he set up boundaries for the peoples
    according to the number of the sons of Israel.
For the Lord's portion is his people,
    Jacob his allotted inheritance.

In a desert land he found him,
    in a barren and howling waste.
He shielded him and cared for him;
    he guarded him as the apple of his eye,
like an eagle that stirs up its nest
    and hovers over its young,
that spreads its wings to catch them
    and carries them on its pinions.
The Lord alone led him;
    no foreign god was with him.

He made him ride on the heights of the land
    and fed him with the fruit of the fields.
He nourished him with honey from the rock,
    and with oil from the flinty crag,
with curds and milk from herd and flock
    and with fattened lambs and goats,
with choice rams of Bashan
    and the finest grains of wheat.
You drank the foaming blood of the grape.

Jeshurun grew fat and kicked;
    filled with food, he became heavy and sleek.
He abandoned the God who made him
    and rejected the Rock his Saviour.
They made him jealous with their foreign gods
    and angered him with their detestable idols.

They sacrificed to demons, which are not God—
  gods they had not known,
  gods that recently appeared,
  gods your fathers did not fear.
You deserted the Rock, who fathered you;
  you forgot the God who gave you birth.

The Lord saw this and rejected them
  because he was angered by his sons and daughters.
'I will hide my face from them,' he said,
  'and see what their end will be;
for they are a perverse generation,
  children who are unfaithful.
They made me jealous by what is no god
  and angered me with their worthless idols.
I will make them envious by those who are not a people;
  I will make them angry by a nation that
    has no understanding.
For a fire has been kindled by my wrath,
  one that burns to the realm of death below.
It will devour the earth and its harvests
  and set on fire the foundations of the mountains.

'I will heap calamities upon them
  and spend my arrows against them.
I will send wasting famine against them,
  consuming pestilence and deadly plague;
I will send against them the fangs of wild beasts,
  the venom of vipers that glide in the dust.
In the street the sword will make them childless;
  in their homes terror will reign.
Young men and young women will perish,
  infants and grey-haired men.
I said I would scatter them

and blot out their memory from mankind,
but I dreaded the taunt of the enemy,
   lest the adversary misunderstand
and say, "Our hand has triumphed;
   the Lord has not done all this.'"

They are a nation without sense,
   there is no discernment in them.
If only they were wise and would understand this
   and discern what their end will be!
How could one man chase a thousand,
   or two put ten thousand to flight,
unless their Rock had sold them,
   unless the Lord had given them up?
For their rock is not like our Rock,
   as even our enemies concede.
Their vine comes from the vine of Sodom
   and from the fields of Gomorrah.
Their grapes are filled with poison,
   and their clusters with bitterness.
Their wine is the venom of serpents,
   the deadly poison of cobras.
'Have I not kept this in reserve
   and sealed it in my vaults?
It is mine to avenge; I will repay.
   In due time their foot will slip;
their day of disaster is near
   and their doom rushes upon them.'

The Lord will judge his people
   and have compassion on his servants
when he sees their strength is gone
   and no one is left, slave or free.
He will say: 'Now where are their gods,

the rock they took refuge in,
the gods who ate the fat of their sacrifices
    and drank the wine of their drink offerings?
Let them rise up to help you!
    Let them give you shelter!

'See now that I myself am He!
    There is no god besides me.
I put to death and I bring to life,
    I have wounded and I will heal,
    and no one can deliver out of my hand.
I lift my hand to heaven and declare:
    As surely as I live for ever,
when I sharpen my flashing sword
    and my hand grasps it in judgment,
I will take vengeance on my adversaries
    and repay those who hate me.
I will make my arrows drunk with blood,
    while my sword devours flesh:
the blood of the slain and the captives,
    the heads of the enemy leaders.'

Rejoice, O nations, with his people,
    for he will avenge the blood of his servants;
he will take vengeance on his enemies
    and make atonement for his land and people.

I believe that one day there will be revival in our land. Before that, however, things have to happen. The Western world has too much pride. When revival comes, it will be a sad day for the fabric of our society. I believe that it is only when our failures have come home to roost that we will be ready to cry to God for help.

I was struck recently by some things that Douglas

Adams, author of *The Hitch-hiker's Guide to the Galaxy*, had to say on the radio about the importance of science. He said, 'Religion is a good way of not knowing about the world.' He went on to advocate the end of all religious education in schools. Even now, many schools do not talk about the Christian God. Many schools will not allow traditional Christian hymns to be sung, in case they offend people who do not share the Christian heritage. These are interesting times in which we live.

As I said earlier, I believe that a day is coming when it will not be tolerated for Christians to speak up for their faith. There will be persecution of Christians until Christ's return, when the judgment of God will be revealed and people will see their folly.

Deuteronomy 32 is not a psalm, but it is in the tradition of the Psalms. I believe that it has a real message for us today. I am convinced there is a real message that God wants his people—whether members of the Southampton Christian Fellowship, who heard me preach about it, or readers of this book—to hear from this passage.

To get the context of the passage, we need to go back to Deuteronomy chapter 31 verses 19–22:

> *'Now write down for yourselves this song and teach it to the Israelites and make them sing it, so that it may be a witness for me against them. When I have brought them into the land flowing with milk and honey, the land I promised on oath to their forefathers, and when they eat their fill and thrive, they will turn to other gods and worship them, rejecting me and breaking my covenant. And when many disasters and difficulties come upon them, this song will testify against them, because it will not be forgotten by their descendants. I know what they are disposed to do, even before I bring them into the land*

I promised them on oath.' So Moses wrote down this song that day and taught it to the Israelites.

It is interesting that God showed Moses that one way of teaching our children about God is to do it in song. The older I get, the more nostalgic I become. I get a real blessing from singing some of the old hymns like 'There is a green hill far away' or 'Onward Christian soldiers, marching as to war'—though I don't suppose that passes the modern tests of political correctness!

The text says that 'this song will testify against them'. In other words, the song will be a witness within their hearts. Isn't that awesome?

I can still remember the hymns I sang at school. I wasn't a Christian then but, 25 to 30 years later, I still remember them and they are a witness within my heart. What I was taught in Religious Education lessons at school is still in my heart and still guiding my life.

God told Moses that he was going to give him a song which would be a witness for God to future generations. When the people would wander from God's path and 'turn to other gods and worship them, rejecting me and breaking my covenant', the words of the song would be a witness to them.

Perhaps when you became a Christian there were particular songs which revived your spirit, or made your heart soar like an eagle, or held eternal truth for you. Do you know the experience of having maybe strayed from your walk with the Lord and finding yourself walking past a church and they are singing your song? The song is a 'witness against you'—a challenge to you.

I have a confession to make. I have just taken up playing the piano. Some days I get home stressed and I need to chill out, so I sit down by the piano and play through some hymns and spiritual songs which really speak to my heart. Afterwards I come out of the lounge revived and ready to face the world again, because God is back in my life.

In doing this, I allow God to revive my soul but I am also providing a simple witness to my family as they hear me playing worship songs and perhaps putting words to the songs. And as it becomes less likely to happen in schools, it is so much more important that you and I provide that witness at home.

[Readers of this book unfortunately miss out in comparison with the live audience. At this point in the sermon, the preacher moves out of the pulpit and gives the congregation a live rendition of his favourite hymns on the keyboard!]

God said to Moses that when the people got into that land flowing with milk and honey, they would forget their God but they would not forget the witness in their heart.

I want to share a parable with you. It was told in the film called *The Crying Game*, so some of you might remember it. I will call it 'In My Nature'.

Once upon a time, there was a frog and a scorpion, whose domicile was a pond—but the frog stayed on the lilypads which were sheltered by the leaves. The scorpion lived on a road and basked in the sun.

The frog was a compassionate soul and even though he hated the water, whenever a dragonfly, a beetle, or a similar insect fell into the pond, he would dive in and rescue it and carry it on his back to the lilypad where the insect could dry off and fly away when he was ready.

The frog was also an observant fellow and he noticed that whenever another animal came into the scorpion's territory, it was stung for its trouble and inevitably died. One day, the frog asked the scorpion why he killed all his visitors so indiscriminately. 'It's in my nature, dear boy,' replied the scorpion. 'It's in my nature.'

It came to pass that the wind blew and a storm arose and the water swept the scorpion into the pond. 'Help me! Help me!' shouted the scorpion. 'Please help me!' But nobody would listen, as they were afraid of the scorpion. No one would listen, that is, apart from the frog, for he could not bear to see anyone in distress.

'I will help you. I will help you,' said the frog, 'but please promise not to sting me.' 'Why should I sting you, if you save my life? Help me, my friend.' Before the scorpion had finished his sentence, the frog was in the water because he could not resist going to the aid of someone in distress. The scorpion clung to his back as the frog made powerful strokes towards his pad. Then, just seconds from his sanctuary, just moments from his haven, he felt a piercing pain in his shoulder blade.

The frog began to lose orientation. His strength was sapping, mist came over his eyes. He said, 'Why? Why? Why, my friend, did you sting me when I was trying to save your life? Now we shall both die.' 'It's in my nature, dear boy,' replied the scorpion. 'It's in my nature.'

You know, there is so much truth in that. We, in our weakest moments, revert to what is in our nature. The frog could no more not help the scorpion than the scorpion could help stinging his friend. So many times, God looks at us and sees our nature as we sting ourselves— and God is there trying to help us, for that, my friends, is in God's nature.

Then (verse 3) Moses recites the song. Some of the words are very familiar to us from worship songs, such as 'Ascribe greatness to our God'. 'His works are perfect, and all his ways are just. A faithful God who does no wrong, upright and just is he.'

God begins with a statement of his own nature before reminding them of their own nature: 'They have acted corruptly toward him; to their shame they are no longer his children, but a warped and crooked generation.'

Sadly the instruction, 'Ask your father and he will tell you, your elders, and they will explain to you' is no longer true. The older generation are no longer the role models for the younger ones. The older generation are more and more trying to be like their own children. They want to be their children's best friend, rather than their role-model or authority to look up to. God, however, makes his case as to why the people should look up to him.

I like the analogy of God as 'an eagle that stirs up its nest and hovers over its young, that spreads its wings to catch them and carries them on its pinions' (verse 11). We like our comfort zones. We don't like to be challenged, to be pushed to something new. In contrast, the eagle stirs up its young, forces them to move on, to take the risk and fly. God may be saying to us, 'It is time for you to fly, time to come out of the comfort zone, time for you to do it on your own.'

When the eagle starts to fly, inevitably it will struggle and fail. The good news is that the parent is there to swoop down and stop it from falling. That is what God does for us too. When he challenges us to do something, he is there to help us and to pick us up when we fail. God may be saying to us: 'There is a time to sit in a nest and there is a time to learn to fly.' It is in our nature to stray and it is in God's nature to restore us.

Notice the strong language that God uses: '...he was angered by his sons and daughters... they are a perverse generation, children who are unfaithful... They made me jealous... and angered me with their worthless idols.' God says that he will give them up, leave them to their own devices. God gave us rules and regulations, but he says, 'If you don't want to live by them, then get on with it. Go your own way.'

It is unfashionable to say so, but one must ask: is AIDS or the new CJD perhaps the result of God allowing people to get on with doing things their own way? I have to say that I believe there is more to come; we ain't seen nothing yet. But I believe, too, that revival will come when men and women come to the end of themselves, the end of their own understanding.

Even as Christians, we can become lazy in our faith, find other things to do on Sunday, not make the time we used to have to pray and read the Bible. Then something shakes the nest and we come running back to God. So it will be for our society as they rush back to God, having seen that their own paths do not work.

The great writer and scholar, Edward Gibbon, said, 'History is little more than a register of the crimes, follies and misfortunes of mankind.' We are a nation without sense. God knows our nature. He gives us freedom to follow human wisdom, or our own ideas, but the end is destruction.

These are not just idle words but they are words of life and death. Jesus is the Word. What he says is not just words but are our life. When I became a Christian and read the Bible for the first time as a believer, the words became my life. The true God died on a cross so that he could become your life. He took on your sinful nature and gave you his own righteous nature so that each day we can pass on our guilt to Jesus, the lamb who was slain, and live.

Prayer

Heavenly Father, thank you for the opportunity to think about your Word. Thank you that you are so intimately involved with us. You hover over us like an eagle. You care about us, you worry about us. You want to teach us to fly. You set us limits and boundaries for our protection. You leave in our hearts a witness, a voice to draw us closer to you. Your thoughts are for us continuously, to draw us closer to yourself.

Help us to look to you as the author and finisher of our faith. May your Word in us be vibrant and alive. Lord we look to you each day for our daily bread. May we be a witness for you to the wider world. In your holy and matchless name, I pray. Amen

BRF's daily Bible reading notes
New Daylight

New Daylight is published three times a year in January, May and September and contains a Bible reading, comment and prayer for every day. It also contains *The BRF Magazine*, which has details of BRF events, developments, news and resources, as well as articles on the Christian life, the Bible, prayer and spirituality.

New Daylight is available from your local Christian bookshop or, in case of difficulty, direct from BRF.

For more information about BRF's Bible reading notes and the full range of our publications, write to: The Bible Reading Fellowship, Peter's Way, Sandy Lane West, OXFORD OX4 5HG (Tel: 01865 748227; Fax: 01865 773150; E-mail: enquiries@brf.org.uk).

Further information can also be found by visiting our website at www.BRF.org.uk.

Other books by BRF

Introductory Bible Readings

If you don't know the Bible very well, or have never read it before on a regular basis, then these introductory Bible readings could provide you with just what you need. They are also ideal for new Christians, since the writers open up all the essential and basic truths of the Christian life.

The seven weeks of undated, daily readings include a Bible passage (printed out in full), a comment and a prayer or reflection for each day. The notes are written in the style of *New Daylight*, BRF's bestselling daily Bible reading notes.

ISBN 0745935540, £1.50

When You Walk
by Adrian Plass

Company and encouragment for ordinary followers of Jesus who sometimes find the going a bit tough

When You Walk is a rich collection of warm, highly individualistic, sometimes refreshingly maverick responses to familiar and not-so-familiar passages from scripture, that Adrian Plass has contributed to the BRF's *New Daylight* Bible reading notes over the last few years.

The material, organised by Adrian himself, includes a new and substantial preface to each of the eighteen sections in the book. Sections include Getting Lost, Obedience, Passion, Theory and Practice, Reality, Story Power, Heading for Heaven and New Beginnings —crucial areas, not just in what we narrowly term 'the Christian life', but in life itself.

ISBN 0745935524, £7.99